AMERICA'S
CRITICAL
THINKING
CRISIS

AMERICA'S CRITICAL THINKING CRISIS

The FAILURE and PROMISE of Education

STEVEN J. PEARLMAN

AMERICA'S CRITICAL THINKING CRISIS

To request permission, contact that author at:
stevenpearlman@gmail.com
StevenPearlman.com
thecriticalthinkinginitiative.org
TheCriticalThinkingInitiative.org

Because of the dynamic nature of the Internet, any web addresses or links contained in this book may have changed since publication and may no longer be valid. The views expressed in this work are solely those of the author and do not necessarily reflect the views of the publisher, and the publisher hereby disclaims any responsibility for them.

Paperback ISBN: 978-1-7359422-0-9
eBook ISBN: 978-1-7359422-1-6

Edited by Susan Strecker
Cover design by Elizabeth Mills
Layout by Madison Lux

For Samuel.
For all the Samuels.
For the late Tom Cannon.
And go Flaming Arrows!

STEVEN J. PEARLMAN, PH.D.

StevenPearlman.com
TheCriticalThinkingInitiative.org

Steve possesses 30 years of experience in higher education. Even before earning his doctorate at the Indiana University of Pennsylvania, Steve already taught writing and critical thinking at a range of institutions, including one of America's elite colleges. Steve then went on to bring his expertise out of the classroom for institution-wide benefit. He co-founded and directed one of the country's first academic offices specifically focused on campus-wide critical thinking, and co-developed what might be the only academic instrument that unifies the teaching, application, assigning, and assessment of critical thinking. Steve has spent the better part of the last ten years focusing on developing students, faculty, executives, and workspaces on critical thinking. He is the co-founder of The Critical Thinking Initiative, and the co-host of *The Critical Thinking Initiative* and *Smarterer* podcasts. Steve lives in Connecticut with his family and is an avid martial artist. He's also the author of *The Book of Martial Power.*

CONTENTS

FOREWORD

by Dave Carillo, M.A.
Co-Founder, The Critical Thinking Initiative

There are a lot of books written about education these days, and a fair number on critical thinking, but this book is different. It's different because it reveals a truth that educators and non-educators alike need to understand. Most other books lean on anecdotal stories from the classroom, stories about lessons that worked in that classroom, challenges overcome in that classroom. Those books are paced by uplifting anecdotes and tragic ones; they are filled with personal reflection, and they share realizations about how the educator learned to teach. Hopefully, the students learned as well, but those books don't necessarily support that.

But few books include hard research to back their message. And even when those other books lean hard on research, cite key theoretical frameworks, and crunch data, rarely does the nonacademic audience see how that research should materially and pragmatically transform education.

And books specifically focused critical thinking typically embody the same struggles: They might reveal the system that idiosyncratically worked for a single CEO, one filled with all sorts of suggestions that may or may not apply to anyone else. Or the reader gets a book that lists every logical fallacy, every cognitive bias, and every metacognitive error, and then advice to just avoid doing those things.

This book is different. How do I know? I was there for the whole ride as Steve's friend, colleague, and collaborator. And believe me, the battles we fought weren't easy ones. So, when I say that this book brings a new message that it is theoretically sound, and that its heart and soul are found in the classroom, I say that from experience.

This book is different because it fought its way through ten years of work in higher education, thousands of students, educational dogma, eager (and resistant) faculty, and course work across the academic spectrum from first-year writing courses to PhD programs in STEM. In fact, the ongoing argument in education for years has been that critical thinking cannot be taught. It cannot be taught because it cannot be defined, or its too difficult, or too idiosyncratic, or that it takes away from the content of the course, or that it is different in every discipline, or that it depends on knowledge, or that it is too much work, or that.... You name the excuse; we heard it. When we began this work ten years ago, our jobs were linked to our ability to overcome the challenges that others seemed content to leave unsurpassed. Though we could not predict the number of challenges we'd face, we eventually transformed the academic culture of our campus.

Most of all, this book is rare because it uses education, cognitive psychology, and neuroscience to tell a story about critical thinking that will appeal to everyone. This isn't a book for educators; it's a book that everyone interested in critical thinking or young people needs to read. As I write this, the autumn of 2020 is around the corner, and everyone who cares about the United States needs to read what this book has to say.

INTRODUCTION:
THE ROOF IS ON FIRE

Education is not the filling of a pail, but the lighting of a fire.
—W.B. Yeats

Something happened at my high school prom that I'll never forget. It was the end of the night and the DJ played the very last song—*The Roof Is on Fire* by Rock Master Scott & the Dynamic Three. And all of us—*all* of us—got up and joined the chorus:

> *The roof, the roof, the roof is on fire*
> *(We don't need no water, let the motherfucker burn)*
> *(Burn, motherfucker, burn)*

On the surface, we reveled all too childishly at cursing in the presence of our faculty chaperones, not to mention the principal himself, whom, we knew, could exact no penalty on us because we'd be graduated shortly. Despite the pleasure we took in our defiance, so pedestrian was our rebellion that the faculty actually chuckled. They'd fought in wars and burned their bras, so not only did our impishness fail to impress them, I suspect they'd wished we relatively comfortable middleclass suburban kids rebelled more.

But there was something about how everyone chanted that chorus that was not just about cursing. The operative word was never "motherfucker". It was "burn". After a dozen years of education, we, for some reason, basked in the notion of the school burning to the ground. This was the place where, despite any of its shortcomings, we all at some point laughed, made some friends, played sports, performed in a play, sang in a chorus, etc. And yet we took at least some delight in the idea of immolating it.

Now, I don't want to suggest that anyone *really* wanted to see it burn. No one threw a Molotov cocktail at the place. No one was planning any *Heathers* boiler-room bombs. But there we were nevertheless, enthusiastically singing about Sachem High School burning. What was it about Sachem High School, about high school itself, about *education* itself, that made us celebrate the idea of the school burning? What made it "just another brick in the wall"?

I realized upon writing this book that I have devoted most of my adult life to that question and resolving the tension of that moment, which lays in a juxtaposition between two unlikely players. The first, William Butler Yeats, was a pillar of Ireland and a Nobel Prize winning symbolic poet of the early 20th century. The second, *Rock Master Scott & the Dynamic Three,* had claim to the number-five song on *Billboard's Dance Music* chart in 1984. At first glance, the latter hardly seems a match for the former, but the eventual outcome might surprise you.

As for me, I'm a professional pedagogue. Though typically defined as an educator who is particularly strict, I use it here differently. For the purposes of this text, I exercise the more professional denotation of "pedagogue"—someone who for some unholy reason studies research on teaching. I've taught in higher education since I was a grad student at American University in 1992, and for the last ten years served as the Director of Interdisciplinary Writing and Reasoning at a university in the northeast.

My partner in crime, David Carillo, is the "Dave" referenced throughout this text. Together, we were charged with raising critical thinking outcomes across campus. And we *did*. He and I also co-host two podcasts. *The Critical Thinking Initiative* focuses on critical thinking in education, and *Smarterer* offers thinking tips for everyone to apply in daily life.

Returning to Yeats versus Rock Master Scott, if the fire metaphors didn't foreshadow it well enough, here's your spoiler alert: The state of critical thinking in education is apocalyptic. For several reasons, my Sachem classmates were not only justified, but arguably righteous in chanting about the school (metaphorically) burning. But I won't tell you the *real* reason until the last chapter.

But before I levy some brutal critiques of educat*ion*, I need to make one thing very clear: I hold only the deepest respect for educat*ors*. In place of the pay they don't get, the respect they lack, and the accolades they do not receive, educators should warrant our culture's highest honors. They should be any culture's highest nobility. We should step aside and bow as they walk by. To quote Anthony Michael Hall from *The Breakfast Club*, "in the simplest terms, in the most convenient definitions," without educators, there's no one else: no doctors to heal the sick, no engineers to build our bridges, no psychologists to mend marriages, no lawyers to prosecute criminals and defend the innocent, no welders, no astronauts. Therefore, if at times I *seem* critical of educators, please know that it's only the *paradigm* in which they exist, including the constraints and requirements forced on them, that bears my critique.

So, let's get started.

Section I justifies my classmates' affection for the *Rock Master Scott* type of fire: the one where academia burns to the ground. I'll show you why America is failing to develop critical thinkers and better humans overall. I'll show you how education squelches students rather than empowering them. I'll show you how it is a game the students will always win, the educators will always lose, and yet a game in which *everyone* suffers.

Section II shows you what education should be, how it can light Yeats's fire within our students. And I'll show you how it doesn't cost a lot of money, require smart classrooms, or depend on large institutional bureaucracies.

My hope is that you'll finish this book not just appreciating why my classmates and I sang for academia to burn, but that you'll sing with us, maybe in the way you expect, more likely in a way you don't yet. But one way or another, as extreme as it might seem right now, I'm out to show you that my classmates had it right.

SECTION I

Let it Burn

In a word, we may reasonably hope for the virtual abolition of education when I'm as good as you *has fully had its way. All incentives to learn and all penalties for not learning will vanish. The few who might want to learn will be prevented; who are they to overtop their fellows? And anyway, the teachers—or should I say, nurses—will be far too busy reassuring the dunces and patting them on the back to waste any time on real teaching. We shall no longer have to plan and toil to spread imperturbable conceit and incurable ignorance among men. The little vermin themselves will do it for us.*
—C.S. Lewis, *The Screwtape Letters*

IT'S CRITICAL THINKING, STUPID
(PART 1)

Foremost is reason. Reason is nonnegotiable. As soon as you show up to discuss the question of what we should live for (or any other question), as long as you insist that your answers, whatever they are, are reasonable or justified or true and that therefore other people ought to believe them too, then you have committed yourself to reason, and to holding your beliefs accountable to objective standards. If there's anything the Enlightenment thinkers had in common, it was an insistence that we energetically apply the standard of reason to understanding our world, and not fall back on generations of delusion like faith, dogma, revelation, authority, charisma, mysticism, divination, visions, gut feelings, or the hermeneutic parsing of sacred texts.
—Steven Pinker, *Enlightenment Now*[1]

Why, oh, why didn't I take the blue pill.
—Cypher, *The Matrix*

THE BLUE PILL

I begin this book with critical thinking because the importance of thinking, I hope, holds *prima facie* importance. If we fail to cultivate in our young people the ability to reason, if we "fall back on generations of delusion," then our children's hope of a better future tumbles toward oblivion. And if you disagree about thinking's eminence, you really should think about why you *think* otherwise.

As for what critical thinking is, well, that's a very complex question. When Dave and I teach critical thinking academically and corporately, we exercise our specific, research-based concepts for critical thinking, but that's a whole other book in itself. There are many other definitions out there, but parsing through them would become a tediously lengthy affair. For this book's discussion, a broad and inclusive definition of critical thinking suffices, such as any conception of the process used to analyze data, solve problems, generate ideas, identify fallacies, locate flaws, etc. Thus, for the sake of this text, critical thinking can remain broadly conceived.

As for the state of critical thinking, I'm going to start with two bits of good news (and there's plenty of bad coming, so enjoy these morsels while you can):

The first is that *all* of us, students included, are critical thinkers by nature. Research reveals that babies—*babies*—just sixteen months old act "surprised by false information, staring at such speakers longer than those who speak truthfully. Infants occasionally interrupt and overtly correct these false claims."[2] Another study of third and fourth-grade students (eight to ten years old) found that they could understand the "advanced" scientific concept of controlling variables and, furthermore, retained that understanding seven months later.[3] In fact, evolution embedded thinking so deeply in our makeup as *homo sapiens* that when measuring IQ scores versus critical thinking scores, researchers found that "critical thinking had a greater association with real life decisions" than IQ, and that critical thinking "explained variance beyond what was accounted for by intelligence alone."[4] That's a very highfalutin way of saying that smart ain't enough. Smart is nice but it differs from critical thinking, and *critical thinking* matters *more*. Again, *the ability to think critically matters more than raw intelligence.*

The second piece of good news is that, here in America, critical thinking doesn't want for supporters.

In terms of the business community, 95 percent of the CEOs surveyed in 2015 agreed that "a candidate's ability to think critically is more important than his or her major."[5] Indeed.com reports that explicit calls for "critical thinking" in job listings doubled in just five years (2009–2014). And in 2018, high percentages of hiring managers and executives rated "critical thinking/analytic reasoning" as "very important" (84 percent and 78 percent respectively).[6]

The general public agrees too, with about 95 percent of people surveyed agreeing that critical thinking skills are essential in today's world, with comparable agreement that K-12 schools and colleges should *require* critical thinking courses.[7]

Educators concur, too. One study found that 99 percent of faculty rate critical thinking as a "very important" or "essential" skill to be developed as part of an undergraduate education.[8] Another survey found that 83 percent of college faculty "cover critical thinking in their courses."[9]

And, when it comes to the students, you'll be happy to know most feel as though college fulfills its critical thinking obligation, with 92 percent of students reporting their conviction that their undergraduate experience improved their critical thinking abilities.

It might come as no surprise then that perhaps no issue in academia garners more increasing attention than critical thinking. A simple database search revealed a 568 percent increase in articles about "critical thinking in education" per decade since 1986.* Academia's discussion of critical thinking is not just a rising tide, it's a tidal wave.

The problem with tidal waves, unfortunately, is that they're typically triggered by massive seismic events and that they often bring widescale death and destruction. Which brings you to a decision point, one not dissimilar from the one Keanu Reeves faced in *The Matrix*.

Sitting with Morpheus, played by Laurence Fishburne, Keanu faced the now iconic blue-pill/red-pill choice of comfortably remaining in his existing worldview or learning about the *matrix*— what the world really was:

---

* There were just 268 hits from 1986–1995. In the following decade, 1996–2005, that roughly doubled to 533 hits. And that figured tripled *again* from 2006–2015 with 1,790 hits.

> *This is your last chance. After this, there is no turning back. You take the blue pill, the story ends, you wake up in your bed and believe whatever you want to believe. You take the red pill, you stay in Wonderland, and I show you how deep the rabbit hole goes.*
> —Morpheus, *The Matrix*

So, this is your blue-pill/red-pill decision. Thus far, I presented the blue-pill world of critical thinking in America. You can put this book down right now and return to your comfortable life believing that my classmates were wrong to want the school to burn because, in terms of critical thinking, we are literally born to do it. And as I've shown, corporate leaders call for it, educators say they teach it, students say the learn it, and *95* percent of our otherwise oft-contentious populous agrees that it is important.

Or there's the red-pill option, where I "show you how deep the rabbit hole goes."

THE RED PILL

In his 2018 Nelson Mandela lecture, President Obama made it clear that our citizenry *lacks* much needed critical thinking skills. As evidence, he pointed to "the promotion of anti-intellectualism and the rejection of science that leaders who find critical thinking and data somehow politically inconvenient. And, as with the denial of rights, the denial of facts runs counter to democracy, it could be its undoing, which is why we must…insist that our schools teach critical thinking to our young people, not just blind obedience." Obama's words might naturally ring true for many, but if you want harder data about the lack of critical thinking in America, this gets there fast: A simple survey of critical thinking skills among respondents from the general populace found that 44 percent earned an F on basic critical thinking skills in 2017. In 2018, 52 percent earned an F.[10] To be clear: *half the adult U.S. population earned an F on a simple critical thinking test.*

If you want insight into why that's the case, one factor assuredly is that "only 20 percent of parents frequently or daily ask their children to take an opposing view [and] only a third of parents have their children regularly discuss issues without a right or wrong answer."[11]

But what about among the educated? What about college students and recent graduates? Consider the Educational Testing Service's 2015 study of college students, which, at over one-hundred-thousand participants, is one of the larger studies ever conducted. What percentage of students did the study find to be proficient in critical thinking? Would it disturb you to know that just 24 percent—fewer than one in four students!—achieved proficiency in critical thinking? If 24 percent disturbs you, then hold on tightly because the study did *not* find 24 percent of students to be proficient critical thinkers. Nor 20 percent. Nor 15 percent. Nor 10 percent. *The terrifying fact is that a meager 4 percent of students were proficient in critical thinking.*

Four. Percent.

And if that strikes you as surprisingly, shockingly, or perhaps even inconceivably low, then you can take comfort that it is, in fact, one of the lower figures to emerge from critical thinking research. On the other hand, those results are from one of the easiest critical thinking tests.

Other studies aren't exactly hopeful: the book *Academically Adrift*, for example, made big headlines a few years back in its conclusion that most college students cannot think or write very well. Many educators searched for ways to rebuke it. In the process, they landed on some legitimate critiques (as well as some needy rationalizations). But for those of us who'd been following critical thinking outcomes for years, *Academically Adrift* hardly told a new tale, and the only surprising thing was that it finally set off the national smoke alarm about thinking outcomes.

In fact, perhaps the only place where Obama erred in his call for critical thinking was in referring to it as a "21st century skill." It's always been needed. Even back in 1990, *A Nation at Risk* found that students lacked "higher-order intellectual skills," with "less than half of students able to draw an inference and where only about one-in-five could write an effective argument."

Since then, *The Wabash National Study of Liberal Arts Education*; *Measuring Up: The National Report Card on Higher Education (2008)*, the *Futures Project: Policy for Higher Education in a Changing World (2005)*, and more studies than I can list here, all generally agree that education basically fails to build capable critical thinkers. Depending on the study, we *might* be able to claim that as many as one-third of college students can think critically, but that's the typical ceiling. We can debate which study proves most valid, but few studies offer anything resembling positive conclusions, much less encouraging ones.

In fact, some educators admit they don't even try to teach critical thinking. But don't blame them. In K-12, for example, most teachers report that they do not train their students in critical thinking "for one simple reason—there is no time. State education departments mandate that so much material has to be covered that critical thinking cannot be taught…. In order to cover the curriculum, courses must be taught quickly, superficially, and uncritically, the infallible way of boring students."[12]

And at the college level, Dan Berrett captured the need for change rather succinctly in *The Chronicle of Higher Education*, writing that "most people agree that students should learn skills like critical thinking [but] courses aren't set up that way."[13]

Perhaps the most "encouraging" research on critical thinking was a meta-analysis of studies on nursing students, which "estimate[d] the overall effect of college on critical thinking skills" as equivalent to moving students "from the 50th percentile to the 72nd percentile."[14] Yet while the authors claim that's "no small improvement in [their] minds," they also note their "inability to make clear causal conclusions" between the gains in critical thinking and the students' education—they're just not sure education itself actually played any role in improving the outcomes. Putting aside my reservations about the critical thinking tests employed in that study (which were often multiple choice—the worst way to test critical thinking), I tend to think that if four years of college only moves someone from the 50th to the 72nd percentile, it's not only what one researcher called "tragically meager,"[15] it's actually an embarrassing indictment of higher education.

And remember, I said that's among the most favorable studies. From there, it only gets worse.

- "Overall, young people's ability to reason about the information on the Internet can be summed up in one word: *bleak.*" (Stanford History Group, 2016)
- 90 percent of employers rank critical thinking as "very important", but they rate only 28 percent of college graduates as capable critical thinkers, and a mere 16 percent as capable writers. (Partnership for 21st Century Skills)
- Wearable brain monitors show that students produce some of the *lowest brain activity* when in class, even lower than when watching TV, relaxing, or doing chores.[16]
- A 2016 PayScale and Future Workplace report found that 60 percent of the 76,000 executives interviewed believe college graduates lack requisite critical thinking skills.
- The Noel-Levitz Employer Satisfaction Survey in 2010 found that critical thinking was "the academic skill with the second largest *negative gap* between performance satisfaction and expectation."[17]

In addition to all that, you'll find it hard to open an issue of *Forbes, The Wall Street Journal,* or other business publications without seeing an executive calling, thirsting,...*pleading* for stronger critical thinking skills in college graduates. Here are a scant few: *Wanted: Millennials Who Can Think Critically* by John Baldoni; *Bosses Seek Critical Thinking, but What Is That?* by Melissa Korn; *Robots May Be Taking Your Job: Here are the Skills You Need to Survive* by Jeff Desjardins; *What Boards Want from Schools* by Richard Rothstein and Rebecca Jacobsen. (It won't be long, I predict, before major corporations start building their own four-year colleges to develop needed skills in new employees. Some are already developing shorter on-boarding certificate programs to train new employees on needed skills such as critical thinking.)

What those calls make clear is the same thing shown by all the outcomes I listed: American education is failing to deliver on its longstanding promise to teach Americans how to think.

And don't think all other countries are just as bad. Relative to their cohorts in other countries, for example, U.S. millennials ranked eighteenth out of nineteen nations in "problem solving in a technology rich environment."[18] Thus, the notion that American academia produces critical thinkers is nothing more than an illusion—a matrix, if you will, of suppositions about pedagogies, subjects, and outcomes. The critical thinking outcomes from our schools are abysmal and business leaders know it.

Thus, to conclude our first step down the dark rabbit hole, the message to educational institutions from corporate America is the same one from Pinker and Obama. And it is the same one we need to sound. It's a call for critical thinking. It's a clear, unambiguous, and definitive cry. If you recall James Carville's famous phrase from the 1992 election—"It's the economy, stupid"—a maxim proven true in every election since—then perhaps you'll appreciate that I'm appropriating it for education as follows. When it comes to what America needs,

It's critical thinking, stupid.

It all comes down to that.

"ANYONE? ANYONE?"

*"In 1930, the Republican-controlled House of Representatives, in
an effort to alleviate the effects of the...Anyone? Anyone...the Great
Depression, passed the...Anyone? Anyone? The Tariff bill? The
Hawley-Smoot Tariff Act? Which, anyone? Raised or lowered?...Raised
tariffs in an effort to collect more revenue for the federal government.
Did it work? Anyone? Anyone know the effects? It did not work, and the
United States sank deeper into the Great Depression. Today we have
a similar debate over this. Anyone know what this is? Class? Anyone?
Anyone? Anyone seen this before? The Laffer Curve. Anyone know
what this says? It says that at this point on the revenue curve, you will
get exactly the same amount of revenue as at this point. This is very
controversial. Does anyone know what Vice President Bush called this
in 1980? Anyone? Something-d-o-o economics. "Voodoo" economics."*
–Ferris Bueller's Day Off

Academic culture, corporate culture, American culture—it's all
awakening to academia's shortfalls in teaching critical thinking. And
a recent panoply of texts has emerged as a result. You might notice
a theme in their titles: *Beyond the University: Why Liberal Education
Matters* by Michael S. Roth (President of Wesleyan University); *The
Fuzzy and the Techie: Why the Liberal Arts Will Rule the Digital World* by
Scott Hartley; *A Practical Education: Why Liberal Arts Majors Make Great
Employees* by Randall Stross, and *In Defense of a Liberal Education* by
Fareed Zakaria. And for every one book, you could find at least fifty
or so articles on the same theme. Just a few of the titles from *Forbes*
alone include George Anders's *That 'Useless' Liberal Arts Degree has
Become Tech's Hottest Ticket*; William Dix's *A Liberal Arts Degree is More*

11

Important than Ever; Renee Morad's *Why Mark Cuban Believes Liberal Arts is the Future of Jobs,* and Natalie Sportelli's *Liberal Arts Majors are 'The Most Desirable Employees': Boom Brands Talk Road to Millennial Success.*

Why all the sudden attention to the liberal arts and humanities? Because circa 1990, some valley in Cali discovered that silicon sells better than wine, so it STEM-bombed American education with a pressure wave that blew out windows as far as the University of Maine. Given the tech boom, the American Academy of Arts & Sciences' analysis showed a 20 percent decline in humanities degrees between 1991 and 2015,[19] with just 6.1 percent of all conferred bachelor's degrees in 2014 being in the humanities, the lowest since 1948. The *National Center for Education Statistics* notes a similar decline in humanities degrees, seeing instead rising numbers of STEM degrees, as well as degrees in health professions and "parks, recreation, leisure and fitness studies."[20] If you're like me, you're wondering right now why you didn't major in "leisure studies."

In what we might think of as "write flight," everyone fled the liberal arts into majors with direct trajectories to jobs, a not-unreasonable move on face value given the debt that follows a bachelor's degree. But did the abandonment of liberal arts live up to its promise? A 2008 *Wall Street Journal* study found that liberal arts majors see the highest growth in their salaries over ten years, often eventually earning more than their non-humanities counterparts.[21] While engineering majors often earn a higher starting salary just out of college, it's the liberal arts majors who are earning more down the road. In *The Fuzzy and the Techie*, Hartley references a 2015 *LinkedIn* study that found that "liberal arts grads are joining the tech workforce more rapidly than technical grads."[22] Hartley also lists some great examples of liberal arts success stories, such as how PayPal cofounder Peter Thiel "studied philosophy and law, and his co-founder of Palantir, CEO Alex Karp, earned a law degree and then a Ph.D. in neoclassical social theory. Ben Silbermann [Pinterest]…studied political science…airbnb cofounders Joe Gebbia and Brian Chesky earned Bachelor of Fine Arts degrees…the cofounder of Salesforce, Parker Harris, studied English literature…and YouTube CEO Susan Wojcicki studied history and literature."[23]

But most of the liberal arts banner waving by tech and corporate leaders doesn't just focus on jobs. Corporate leaders also advocate for how well the liberal arts cultivate critical thinking. Michael S. Roth, President of Wesleyan University, makes a nice case for it in *Beyond the University: Why Liberal Education Matters*, when he contends that "the demand that we replace broad contextual education meant to lead to lifelong learning with targeted vocational undergraduate instruction is a critical mistake, one that neglects a deep American tradition of humanistic education that has been integral to our success as a nation and that has enriched the lives of generations of students by enhancing their capacities for shaping themselves and reinventing the world they will inhabit."[24]

In a similar remark, Zakaria quotes Edgar Bronfman, former CEO of Seagram Company, and his advice to young people: "Get a liberal arts degree. In my experience, a liberal arts degree is the most important factor in forming individuals into interesting and interested people who can determine their own paths through the future…. For all the decisions young business leaders will be asked to make based on facts and figures, needs and wants, numbers and speculation, all of those choices require one common skill: how to evaluate raw information, be it from people or a spreadsheet, and make reasoned critical decisions."

Like Bronfman's call for "reasoned critical decisions," many calls for the liberal arts, indeed in every source referenced above, speak in one way or another to how the liberal arts foster essential "fundamental skills—critical thinking, reading comprehension, logical analysis, argumentation, clear and persuasive communication,"[25] as well as the capacity to work well with others and the ability to see a broader picture. Indeed, Christian Madsbjerg's entire book, *Sensemaking*, argues for why strong decision making must move beyond data to account for denser ecosystems of culture, intuition, creativity, and *phronesis*—Aristotle's concept of practical wisdom. Madsbjerg details how master *sensemakers* such as Warren Buffet can triumph beyond technical data calculations, and, like the others here, Madsbjerg advocates for a rich education akin to liberal arts.

As a liberal arts educator myself, you'll find no argument from me against the value of the liberal arts overall, the extent to which they've been foolishly devalued since the space race, or the extent to which our politically contentious society needs them now more than ever. But even though the liberal arts should serve an *unquestionable* role in *every single student's* career, I will tell you as a professional pedagogue that when it comes to teaching thinking, the liberal arts solve almost nothing.

Yes, reading Shakespeare or Frost, or Heidegger or Lao Tzu, or studying the Enlightenment is valuable. It's so valuable, in fact, that as my favorite professor from American University, the late Tom Cannon said, we should "keep good books in our medicine cabinets" for they should heal our ailments—the philosophical, sociological, sexual, relational, etc. "If a book doesn't help you on your next date," Tom admonished, "throw it out." Don't take "date" too literally here (but don't discount it either); Tom more broadly contended, and rightfully, that if Wordsworth should warrant even a word's worth of reading, his writings—all writings—must improve our ability to understand and advance the human condition. They must help us reason through our daily lives. And when it comes to the advancement of the human condition, the liberal arts prove invaluable.

Sort of.

The ineluctable point Tom missed was that even the most sapient text, if taught poorly, might just as well be a tome of random glyphs. Therefore, while I would generally argue that students should, in fact, study the liberal arts, the *mere* inclusion of liberal arts study, in and of itself, fails to elevate students into better thinkers.* What the calls

---

* It's deeper than that though. Just reading novels, for example, a part of liberal arts that might not be a part of chemistry, increases our capacity for empathy and makes us look at that world in new ways. But that's not the same as *teaching* thinking. Not at all.

for reinvigorating liberal arts education miss is that *subject matter never holds primacy in education.* I've worked with educators across education's entire expanse, and I can assure you that, as Lisa Tsui concluded from her research, "the development of critical thinking is more influenced by instruction…[and that] progress in this cognitive area is not bound by the type of course in which one enrolls but rather is more greatly affected by the mode of instruction that one encounters in his or her courses."[26]

Subject matter doesn't really matter. Rather, education's *non plus ultra* of power comes in a single word: *pedagogy*—teaching method. And when it comes to capturing the power of pedagogy, no one did it better, albeit inadvertently, than Marshall McLuhan, who famously coined the phrase, "the medium is the message." McLuhan's insight was that *how* we experience media is more important than what the media delivers in content. For example, the fact that TV makes us physically and intellectually passive absorbers of information (as opposed to more active modes such as reading or conversing), is *much* more consequential than whatever information the television delivers.

But McLuhan's maxim translates here perfectly. If the medium is the message then, when it comes to teaching,

The pedagogy is the lesson.

Put another way, in education, the pedagogy is the signal, the subject matter is the noise. There's a critical difference between assigning students a reading about philosophy, science, or education, and teaching them to become philosophers, scientists, and educators. Education favors the former. The world needs the latter. And that all depends not on what we teach, but how.

With respect to the present and misguided emphasis on the *what* instead of the *how,* consider that in thirty years of teaching, nearly everyone who learns that I teach asks *what* I teach. But I easily can sum up the number of times I've been asked, *"How* do you teach?"

None. No one has ever asked me that. *"How* do you teach?" is the most unasked question in academia, and yet the most important.

So how do American teachers teach? Despite what many educators themselves believe, most of the methods employed to foster critical thinking actually don't foster it much…or at all. And some cause more harm than good.

The most insidious culprit of that is lecture, so that's where I begin. The purported good news is that many educators will *claim* they don't lecture, that they favor more progressive, active teaching methods instead. And there's widespread perception in higher education that lecture doesn't dominate teaching. However, I not only can assure you from personal experience that lecture remains ubiquitous, the research shows that any suggestion that "the traditional lecture is dead would be presumptuous."[27] It not only persists in its raw form, but also through a number of newfangled variants, such as "flipped classrooms," where students view videos of lectures, as well as through the use of electronic clickers or phone apps through which students provide real-time feedback on what they're learning.

Such clickers are nice. In limited circumstances, they might serve valuable purposes. For example, if contending with sensitive social or personal issues, such as whether or not students were subjected to racism or sexism, anonymous clicking is great. And it certainly does offer an immediate snapshot of what percentage of the class can name the Hawley-Smooth Tariff Act.

But lecture survives. And it pervades.

What's so *wrong* with lecture? After all, who among us cannot fondly recall at least a few classes with inspiring, certainly thought-provoking lectures? I suspect that you can think back to an enrapturing lecture that provoked you to consider new ideas, a lecture that challenged everything you held sacred, a lecture that "changed your life forever." Can *I* really tell *you* that such a lecture didn't make you think?

I can. You see, even if a lecture succeeds in prompting students to think *about* an interesting idea, it does not teach students *how* to think of their own interesting idea. Receiving even the most mind-blowing idea still differs entirely from being taught how to develop one, or how to ask the provocative question, or how to reason through multifaceted layers of evidence, or how to bring forward such innovative ideas that students will someday hear a lecture about *your* work.

Worse, lecture not only fails to foster thinking, *lecture actually suppresses it* because the mind becomes habituated to the stimulus of the talking head. *Habituation*—the dulling of the mind to stimuli through repetition—suppresses the mind's natural inclination to think, and neuroscientific explorations of education tell us that "nothing demonstrates habituation more than lecture."[28] Lecture's "traditional didactic approach...tends to focus on the back cortex"[29] of the brain—the part that memorizes stuff—but doesn't involve the brain's front cortex—*the part that thinks*. Because lectures "do not teach to both the back and front cortex," neuroscientists call them "unjust,"[30] which, as you'll come to see, puts it mildly.

To understand the severity of the problem, you need to know that a part of our brains called the *basal ganglia* plays an important role in what we experience as pleasurable. When stimulated, the *basal ganglia* releases dopamine, one of our natural pleasure drugs; it makes us find an experience pleasurable. As it turns out, and this should come as no surprise, the *basal ganglia* becomes stimulated and releases dopamine when we engage in critical thinking. Why does the brain like thinking? Because if our brains didn't evolve to enjoy thinking then non-thinkers would have dominated our evolutionary past, which would have resulted in the biggest technological advancement of 2020 being something like a pointier wooden spear.

Therefore, we evolved to enjoy thinking. But guess what doesn't stimulate the *basal ganglia:* lecture. When it comes to tasks such *as rote memorization,*[31] the *basal ganglia* doesn't get involved. So, if students seem bored by being told a bunch of information by some talking head, that's because their brains evolved to find that boring. If you want some evidence for that, consider that at any given moment during a lecture, about 40% of students report that they aren't paying attention.[32] No matter how *seemingly* engaging the lecture (and I'll discuss later why engaging lectures really aren't much better than unengaging ones), it largely activates only the rear cortex, prohibiting the pre-frontal cortex from doing the more interesting work of making meaning and thinking. (I should parenthetically note here that I don't believe lecture holds *no* place in academia or in the intellectual world. Occasionally, once in a while, a good lecture can be great. But only when it is the exception rather than the rule, which it presently is not.)

In fact, and the implications of this next study should horrify you, one experiment[33] introduced children to a new toy in three different ways: Children were either (1) taught how to use it through demonstration, i.e., lecture, (2) taught by watching a presenter explore some different aspects of the toy, i.e., another lecture, or (3) just handed the toy and given the opportunity to go at it. Out of the three groups of children, those taught how to use the toy ultimately played with it *less* than the other groups. Being lectured to about how to use the toy *reduced* children's engagement of the toy.

If lecture's suppression of engagement doesn't make you uncomfortable enough, neuroscience points to the fact that lectures actually "hurt"[34] and can even "*damage the brain*."[35] That damaging effect emerges from one of the brain's greatest strengths: its *neuroplasticity*. It is "evident," neuroscientists tell us, "that what we pay attention to each and every day literally changes the structure and function of our brain,"[36] which means that paying attention to lecture builds all the *wrong* neural pathways: pathways for sitting passively and quietly, pathways for memorizing information without thinking about it, and pathways suppressing needs to move around or think for oneself. Since students are "literally strengthening...or weakening the synaptic connections between the neurons of their brains" during every single experience in their lives, the prevalence of lecture means education is constantly building unhappy brains that are equipped to memorize information but ill-equipped to think about it critically.

The brain's painful experience during lecture lashes out through some of the so-called "behavioral problems" we see in students.

Under "sustained boredom," such as when the *basal ganglia* flatlines during lectures, the pre-frontal cortex, which engages in higher-order thinking and *behavior regulation*, literally "loses connection with the rest of the brain."[37] To repeat, when bored, the thinking part of the brain, the part that governs behavior, "loses connection with the rest of the brain." Once that connection is lost, the pre-frontal cortex *cannot* do what it is designed to do—the meaningful work of "judgement, goal-directed planning, risk assessment, attention focus, distraction suppression, and intentional control over emotional responses."[38]

Thus, the daydreamers and doodlers, the raucous and the rebellious, the frustrated and furious, might only *appear* behaviorally challenged. Some students who appear to struggle with learning deficiencies, including "cognitive limitations" and "lack of effort,"[39] might not be behaviorally deficient at all. What's *really* happening to many of those students is that lecture actually prevents their thinking-brains from functionally regulating their behavior. They *can't* regulate their behavior during class, *can't* engage subject matter, *can't* determine their goals, etc. Evolution made their brains frustrated-by-design at the relative oppression of being in a situation where they cannot *think for themselves*. Lectures not only fail to develop the brain, they arguably torture it, which means that *some* of those "problem" students are arguably the ones in their right minds, if not the smarter ones.

Despite lecture's failings overall, some students will tell us that they sometimes enjoy lecture, especially one by an entertaining or engaging lecturer. In fact, students *erroneously* believe that they learn more from lectures than they actually do, and that's especially true of lectures by "a superstar lecturer."[40] The lecture *seems* to work, but when tested, the students actually learn far less than they report.

So, students grossly overestimate how much they learn from superstar lectures. And for that reason, and others, students may embrace lecture and *initially* resist education that calls upon them to be more active.[41] Students rate "the quality of instruction in passive lectures more highly [than active learning]…even though their scores on independent tests of learning were lower than those in actively taught classrooms."[42] In other words, students erroneously think "good" lectures teach them more than other, more active kinds of learning. Why? Why do students favor passive learning? Why do they welcome the doldrum of lecture? For two reasons, and I'll develop these in more depth as the book moves forward.

First, remember that the educational system spent years building their brains with neural pathways that like passively receiving information; they've been raised in lecture, and their brains reflect that. Second, given the kind of testing students will face, lectures can be the most expedient means to what is a highly flawed end—a test that measures their recall of information rather than their ability to think about it. So, yes, many students will "want" lecture, but only in the way smokers want cigarettes. They've become addicted to them. They're an efficient means to a fowl goal. That doesn't make them healthy.

Yet, rather than close out this discussion of lecture with another inundation of modern research, I want to take you back to 1951 and show you, as Herbert Schueler pointed out back then, that none of what I've said here is really all that new:

> *Learning succeeds to the degree that the learner feels that what he is learning matters to him and to the degree that he is actively engaged in the process. Neither factor is effective without the other; learning is their product, not their sum. While it may be possible for the student to achieve a significant degree of motivation by the contagion of a lecturer's enthusiasm for his subject and his skill in arousing interest, it is difficult to see how any series of lectures, no matter how skillfully conceived and delivered, can consistently evoke sufficient student activity to justify their regular use. In a form lecture situation, the lecturer, let us give him the benefit of the doubt, is the one truly active person in the room; therefore he, and not any one of his students, is the one who is learning the most. His students are spectators of the learning process, rather than participants in it.*

You might think academia found ample time to reconstruct learning in the seventy years since Schueler's critique. But sadly, it did not; lecture remains commonplace. But it's certainly not the only teaching method. Many educators do incorporate or rely on other pedagogies.

The question, however, is whether or not newer methods do a better job of cultivating thinkers. (Spoiler: They don't.)

HOPEFUL PEDAGOGIES

Given the failings of lecture as a teaching method, it becomes even more important that you understand the "better" pedagogies faculty use in its place. To that end, the *Instructor Engagement Insights* (IEI) survey of faculty by Cengage Learning provides us with an excellent place to start. And the first thing that the IEI tells us is that "83 percent of the responding instructors" report that they "cover critical thinking in their courses." Eighty-three percent isn't bad but note that one-in-five responding educators just openly admitted that they frankly just *don't* cover critical thinking at all. If you do not find that outright appalling, then I don't know how else to phrase it to change your mind—maybe something like, *"almost 1 in 5 educators are comfortable enabling the intellectually dull?"*.

But what if I were to tell you that when it comes to academia's failings, the 17 percent of educators who admittedly don't teach critical thinking aren't the most insidious? More insidious than the 17 percent who know that they don't teach thinking are the 83 percent who believe they do. Whereas the 17 percent know what they're *not* accomplishing, we cannot say the same for the 83 percent. See, the IEI really does *not* show that 83 percent of faculty "cover critical thinking"; it only shows that 83 percent *believe* that they cover critical thinking.

To appreciate the gaping chasm between their belief and the reality, you need to know that the top four teaching methods the instructors reported using to "cover critical thinking" are *group discussion, case studies, reading questions,* and *online discussion.* Now those might sound like methods that would work. How, you might wonder, could an engaging discussion about a complex idea *not* cultivate critical thinking?

The answer roots in the fact that all four methods mentioned constitute *immersion methods* of teaching critical thinking.[43] *Immersion methods* operate on the premise that engaging students in interesting experiences, such as an interesting discussion, transforms students into better critical thinkers. This comfortable idea widely permeates academia. In fact, *academia at all levels might foremost predicate itself on this fallacy: If we immerse students in something interesting, thoughtful, complex, etc., then that immersion will teach them how to think.*

Unfortunately, relative to *direct methods* of teaching thinking, *immersion* methods accomplish the *least* when it comes to actually improving students' critical thinking. (When immersion methods do suggest gains, they only do so because of *other* pedagogies employed around them, pedagogies I'll discuss in Section II). In short, *immersion* teaching methods—the most common methods other than lecture—don't teach students to become better critical thinkers.

To give you a more specific insight into the failure of immersion methods to teach critical thinking, consider a study[44] that divided students into two groups: One group learned by lecture, which, as we now know, not only fails at teaching thinking but also "hurts." The other group experienced *the number one method the IEI respondents used for critical thinking:* group discussion. The study found "no significant difference on the [critical thinking] performance of the two instructional groups." For all intents and purposes, group discussion failed to teach critical thinking any better than lecture, which doesn't teach critical thinking at all. Simply put, educators need to understand that if students are going to "transition from being inclined to thinking critically to actually having the skill," they need to do more than just immerse students in intellectual ideas. They need to actually teach students how to think.

Unfortunately, where this whole situation becomes even more bleak—so much bleaker—is that when asked for individual narrative accounts of what they specifically *do* in order to actually *teach* critical thinking, the educators in the IEI responded as follows:

- "I do not TEACH critical thinking per se, I just use the topics of the texts we are reading in class to raise certain questions that force them to go further in their analysis."
- "I don't believe it can be explicitly taught—it must be modeled in the context of the class material...I teach physics, so clear examples, lab activities, and good homework questions are important."
- "I don't teach the process of critical thinking in class, but I present students with experiences and activities that require them to think critically."
- "I start every semester telling students to question everything they hear on the news, in their classes, and from me. I remind them of this throughout the semester."
- "I think it comes natural in the content of the courses for communication. That is, while the form may change a bit, it's still the same principle. It's careful listening–not necessarily negative, ambushing listening, but careful attention to personal narratives, media ideas, and/or scholarly insights. So, I'm not sure I really "decide to teach it"—it just is part of the course naturally."
- "In my courses, I teach nursing students. They have to learn to think on their feet and apply concepts they've learned about physiology and therefore have to be able to process information analytically and then act on it."
- "...I regularly begin my topics with questions to determine what they know ahead of introducing the topic; that is designed to get their critical thinking 'juices' going."
- "When we are involved in the discussion of an important issue or when I ask them to write about some topic, I will require them to address the issue or topic in a manner that indicates that they are covering several aspects of that issue."

The first response captured it best for all of them. When asked what they do to teach critical thinking, they confessed that, in actuality, they *"do not* teach critical thinking, per se,"* which means that they actually don't teach it at all. Contrary to what the educators assert, critical thinking skills don't improve by telling students to "question everything". (Asking "how much wood *could* a woodchuck chuck if a woodchuck *could* chuck wood?" doesn't really make us smarter.) Critical thinking also doesn't "come natural in the content of the courses for communication." And "critical thinking 'juices'" simply aren't a thing.

The "good" news, though, is that when pressed, what the responses above reveal is that many educators are self-aware about the fact that they don't really *teach* students to think critically. And perhaps no study advances our discussion of the simultaneous desire for, yet dearth of, critical thinking education better than one from the *International Journal for the Scholarship of Teaching and Learning* titled, *A Hopeful Pedagogy to Critical Thinking.*[45] Its title suggests the authors discovered some way that educators actually *do* teach thinking, some kind of "hopeful" Holy Grail for teaching thinking.

But the authors employ the title as a masterful play on words. Their research didn't find a pedagogy with "hopeful" outcomes at all. It found just the opposite. It found that when it came to teaching critical thinking, educators could only express "hope" that students became better at it:

> "Well, hopefully [the students] become wiser."

> "It is hopefully learned."

> "Our job is to teach them the knowledge they need and *hopefully* they can take that and use it in critical thinking out in the real world."

If only hoping made it so. But reviewing the research thus far, lecture hurts; the top methods educators employ for teaching critical thinking don't work; when pressed for how they actually "teach" critical thinking, educators admit that they do not, and educators confess they *hope* students learn to think critically, but can't say they do.

Of course, not all educators content themselves with being hopeful. Some devote a lot of energy to pedagogies that *do* purportedly develop critical thinking skills. Such "deep" teaching methods, such as active learning (getting students *doing* their learning), flipped classrooms (moving lectures outside class), and collaborative learning (group projects), do hold real potential. But such methods do not *necessarily* produce positive outcomes. In fact, they more typically fail. As some research has concluded, there is actually "a lack of connection between" those deeper approaches "and critical thinking skills."[46]

One reason is that, as one study revealed, not one out of thirty educators could give "a clear idea of critical thinking;"[47] they could only offer a "a dog's breakfast" definition—a hodgepodge of miscellaneous terms and catch phrases, including but not limited to "some mix of reasoning, argument analysis, introductory formal logic, informal logic, inductive reasoning, critical thinking, problem-solving and/or decision making."[48]

Another reason deeper learning approaches fail hinges on the fact that "active learning"—the umbrella-term for learning in which students are working agents rather than passive recipients—is so nebulous that what makes "it" an effective practice becomes nearly impossible to quantify. It's not that active learning strategies can't work. They can. But for them to work, they *require* that certain factors and forces are in place, and most educators lack training in those factors and forces.

For example, many educators try to integrate active learning with lecture, but do so in the wrong order. They lecture first, as a primer for students about the material, and then send students to engage in more active learning experiences. But research shows us that "if you have a lecture first and [students] haven't explored the problem by [themselves] a little bit," active learning exercises typically fail. The active learning needs to come first not only because it sets the precedent that students will be the active agents of learning, but because when lecture precedes active engagement, students "don't even know what questions the lecturing is answering."[49]

That's just one example out of *dozens* about the precarious nature of employing active learning techniques. As another example, multiple research studies provide overwhelming evidence that even the professor's intellectual demeanor mitigates the extent to which students *really* become active. Professors need to model traits such as intellectual humility, curiosity, critical thinking, *un*certainty, a desire to learn, openness to new ideas, etc. If not, the educator who assigns active learning but doesn't *model* active learning, undermines his or her noble goal to engage students actively.

Therefore, it should come as no surprise that students and faculty differ about how much active learning really happens. One study by the National Center for Postsecondary Improvement at Stanford University found the following differences in how students and faculty perceived education:

	Faculty	Students
Design classes to be highly interactive	58.6%	21.3%
Encouragement of student involvement in the classroom	78.9%	28.8%
Use of active learning techniques	63.9%	8.6%
Encourage student collaboration	75.7%	20.7%
Depend on same teaching routines year after year	12.1%	25.3%

Clearly, at least as far as the students *perceive* it, education isn't very active at all. But I'll step in one more time here to reiterate that educators deserve absolutely no blowback for this. They lack the time to steep themselves in this research, and they lack sufficient training from nerds like me who do steep themselves in it. The vast majority of educators are out there fighting the good fight, and they need support, not criticism.

However, if we really want to foster the skills clamored for in *Beyond the University: Why Liberal Education Matters*; *The Fuzzy and the Techie: Why the Liberal Arts Will Rule the Digital World*; *A Practical Education: Why Liberal Arts Majors Make Great Employees*, and *In Defense of a Liberal Education*, then we need to do much more than just shepherd students back into liberal arts classes (though we should do that too). If we are going to foster traits such as "intellectual curiosity and confidence, creativity, strong interpersonal communication, empathy for others, and a love of learning and problem solving,"[50] then we need to remember that *the pedagogy is the lesson*. We can assign the richest texts in the world, books that are "medicine" indeed, books that should help students "on their next date," but if educators lack training in research-based teaching practices that foster real engagement and critical thinking, then what are we really accomplishing by teaching students about the Hawley-Smoot Tariff Act?

Anyone? Anyone?

0.65 PERCENT

Even though no one *needs* to write in order to think critically, when it comes to teaching and assessing critical thinking, nothing does it better than writing. In fact, researchers deemed that "writing is the key pedagogy distinguishing institutions with strong critical thinking versus institutions with low critical thinking."[51] That's so important that I'm going to repeat it: *"writing* is the key pedagogy distinguishing institutions with strong critical thinking versus institutions with low critical thinking."

I'll regale you with the research on writing's power in Section II, but for now, Fareed Zakaria does a good job in layperson terms of summing up the writing-thinking connection: "When I begin to write, I realize that my 'thoughts' are usually a jumble of half-formed ideas strung together, with gaping holes between them. It is the act of writing that forces them out."[52]

Given, therefore, that writing can transform "half-formed ideas" into cogent thoughts, you might think that educators effectively leverage writing all the time. Unfortunately, American education generally fails to employ writing effectively. In fact, "there may often be little, if any, relationship between writing and critical thinking. Courses...taught by faculty who believe that they are in fact eliciting those abilities, nevertheless [fail] to do so."[53]

Wait a minute. Doesn't that contradict the earlier point that *"writing* is the key pedagogy distinguishing institutions with strong critical thinking versus institutions with low critical thinking"? Unfortunately not.

The problem is that even though many educators assign writing, and even though many will laud writing's importance, the mere presence of *some kind* of writing doesn't necessitate any critical thinking. When writing is employed in middle and high schools, for example, it is more typically in what are called, *writing to learn* contexts, which typically involves writing to acquire information. But that's not at all the same thing as writing to compose an idea, i.e., writing to *think*. In fact, one study found that middle and high school writing involved "note taking while listening (91 percent of teachers), short answer response (78 percent of teachers), completing a worksheet (74 percent of teachers), writing an explanation (74 percent of teachers), note taking while reading (69 percent of teachers), analysis/interpretation (68 percent of teachers), writing a description (64 percent of teachers), summary writing (61 percent of teachers), and writing a list (52 percent of teachers)."[54]

Writing to learn is wonderful and should be used *more,* which is supported by a recent meta-analysis of sixty-six studies that found that writing about reading assignments positively impacted students' reading comprehension and other learning outcomes 94 percent of the time.[55] But that kind of writing still doesn't necessarily improve critical thinking, and out of all of the uses of writing described above, only one, "analysis/interpretation," directly called for critical thinking.

But it gets worse. Out of "8,542 separate assignments" researchers gathered from 138 middle and high school students across English, science, social science/history, and math, "only 19 percent represented extended writing of a paragraph or more; all the rest consisted of fill in the blank and short answer exercises, and copying of information directly from the teacher's presentation."[56] Only 19 percent were a paragraph or more! And that's what they called "extended" writing. And the same study found that English classes devoted a paltry 6.3 percent of class time to the "teaching of explicit writing strategies."

But other countries do it better. In fact, "writing plays a more significant role in the school systems in countries that score high" on the Programme for International Student Assessment, which tests students' skills internationally, "than it does in the schools in the United States."[57] That fact led the researchers to conclude that writing is "a frighteningly low priority in U.S. schools." (But don't you dare blame teachers for this. There's ample research that they are too burdened by looming standardized tests and large class sizes to effectively invoke writing in their teaching, especially since most of them need more training in how to do so.)

Unfortunately, though I've spoken to junior high and high school outcomes so far, the use of writing doesn't get much better at the college level. In *The Neglected "R": The Need for a Writing Revolution*, the College Board's National Commission on Writing in America's Schools and Colleges found that "analyzing arguments and synthesizing information are...beyond the scope of most first-year [college] students."[58] Perhaps that's because, as one of the larger studies ever done discovered, roughly two-thirds of all the writing assignments in higher education only ask students to summarize.[59] Consider that. Two-thirds of the assignments that students encounter *in college* only ask them to synopsize the ideas *someone else* already thought.

Is that emphasis on summary *always* bad? Not always. Summary, and its cousin, synthesis—the combining of multiple sources into a narrative—sometimes serve important functions. For example, the doctor getting a drug synopsis from a pharmacist only needs to know which drug the pharmacist recommends, its risks, potential interactions with other drugs, etc. That doctor doesn't need to know, and lacks the time to read, a painstakingly detailed account of the pharmacist's reasoning process about dozens of research studies on the many potentially viable drugs for the patient.

Similarly, you, my good reader, really do not want the extended version of this text that would include how I reasoned through thousands of studies, weighing evidence and methodology as I did so, to provide you with this final synthesized narrative about the critical thinking problem. That text would be ten times longer than this one and would require in-depth discussions of learning theories that only interest pedagogues. Put another way, such a text would bore you to death.

Texts for general audiences need to be written accordingly, which is why a book such as Brian Greene's *The Elegant Universe* offers a wonderfully digestible discussion of physics for the layperson. Greene doesn't delve into proving points through advanced theoretical mathematics. He also doesn't parse his way through advanced papers on physics. And he glosses over many points that serious physicists would debate. But non-physicists like me wouldn't understand his book if he didn't, so Greene did exactly what he needed to do for the audience he needed to reach.

In such cases, summary and synthesis serve important purposes, and they come with the presumption that their authors, such as expert pharmacists or physicists or, hopefully here, pedagogues, are capable of and have exercised considerable reasoning in order to produce end-user texts.

But that's not what we want from writing in academia (or business), not when students should be learning how to think critically. What we want in academia is the *opposite* of the kind of writing I referenced above. We want academia to teach the kind of writing that forces students to develop complex critical thinking skills, the kind of writing suited *not* for laypersons but for experts. Students could then, when needed, parse their thinking down for the layperson, but students who can only write for the layperson cannot magically escalate and complicate their thinking when needing to execute intellectually heavy work.

That heavy work begins with assignments, which, as I mentioned earlier, typically fail to ask for critical thinking. But assignments, though the most visible layer of the problem, represent the symptom rather than the cause. The real reason writing fails is that even though the study of writing for critical thinking "has increased steadily internationally, and domestically in other disciplines," it has "fizzled out in U.S. English departments where the majority of [writing teachers] are employed."[60] Or, as another author put it, "individual cognition," i.e., *critical thinking,* "as a focus of inquiry within [American] composition, took a back seat" to other considerations long ago.[61] In other words, American writing professors have stopped focusing on writing as a critical thinking act, focusing instead on writing as a means to other ends.

What are those other ends? A recent mega-survey of 457 higher-education first-year writing programs by Swarthmore[62] shows us. The question was, "what is the content in first-year composition?"* Here's the breakdown of responses:

- 291 emphasized "Genre/Modes" [different forms of writing]
- 264 emphasized "Themes" [such as "identity" or "diversity"]
- 223 emphasized "writing about writing" [learning about writing theory]
- 157 emphasized "Writing Across the Curriculum/Topic Based" writing
- 135 emphasized "literature"
- 146 emphasized "other"

Out of the 146 institutions that answered "other," *three* specifically listed critical thinking. Three. About another three cited "analysis"; about a dozen used the term "argument", and about a seventeen could only throw their arms in the air and confess that the emphasis just "varied widely" by instructor.

But let me return to the fact that out of 457 institutions, *three*, or 0.65 percent, explicitly focus on "critical thinking." Most of the 457 institutions, I'm *sure*, would pound their tables about how critical thinking naturally emerges as a function of writing instruction. And, to be fair, a "mode" such as writing to compare and contrast might also tacitly call for critical thinking. But it also might not. In fact, recent research[63] on college writing concluded, not surprisingly, that the mere presence of writing, no matter the *quantity*, does *nothing* to

---

* The study makes a distinction between "First-Year Composition", "First-Year Writing Seminar", and "First-Year Seminar." I chose First-Year Composition because it is, in theory, most exclusively focused on writing rather than on other institutional aims, whereas first-year seminar, for example, might also focus on helping students adjust to social factors and college culture.

foster critical thinking. Any student good enough to get into a college can generate however-many-pages-of-words educators require for any given assignment, but not necessarily one page that definitively develops a critical thought. Thus, even though I promise you that writing holds eminent *potential* and that writing teachers should be the noblemen and noblewomen of the academy, merely requiring that students produce fonted pages in no way necessitates that a thought is thunk.

(Despite the consternation I feel, and I hope you feel, about the scant amount of explicit emphasis on critical thinking in first-year writing courses, I should note that none of the top three emphases— *themes, writing about writing, literature*—are ignoble. I know and have worked with compositionist colleagues who accomplish meaningful, powerful learning with students in those areas and others. And as I'll advocate later on, *composition and compositionists should serve as one of every educational institution's most valuable commodities.*)

Furthermore, before you judge educators too harshly, it's fair play to ask whether or not *you* ever bullshitted your way through a paper. Or not if you ever bullshitted *one*, but if there were even a few high school or college or graduate-school papers where you didn't bullshit *at all*? Add some padding to meet a page length? Throw in a few extra quotations? Write something that you didn't really care about? Say what you thought the teacher wanted to hear?

I did those things too. I haven't met anyone who hasn't.

And if you did bullshit sometimes, you're hardly alone. In fact, a recent study[64] examined 174 first-year students across sixteen colleges and found that over half the papers included one or more instances of what's known as *patchwriting*, which is basically stealing passages from other writers and quilting them together:

> *When recapitulating the source material, [patchwriters] "borrowed" phrases [from their sources], patched together into "new" sentences; they "borrowed" whole sentences, deleting what they consider irrelevant words and phrases; and they "borrowed" a hodgepodge of phrases and*

sentences in which they changed grammar and syntax, and substituted synonyms straight from Roget's.[65]

The problem with the "borrowed phrases" of patchwriting isn't only that it's bullshit, nor that the use of published language happens to be plagiarism. The most insidious problem with patchwriting is that the patchwriter isn't even really writing, which means the patchwriter certainly isn't thinking.

Unfortunately, even though most writing in academia doesn't involve critical thinking, the "critical thinking" is still *perceived*. In order to earn good grades, students learn to produce writing that teachers find "acceptable,"[66] which is another way of saying that students learn (intentionally or not) to write the things their teachers want to hear, the way their teachers want to hear them. Students learn to write fluent psychology for their psych professor, or fluent philosophy for their philosophy professor, or fluent Kingsley for professor Kinglsey. And when professors see writing that reads more like writing "should" sound in their field, then, consciously or not, they see those students as thinking better. Unfortunately, the evidence shows that students' "internal thinking" actually doesn't change just because they learn to write in forms that mimic professors or disciplinary genres.[67]

To conclude, to say that writing in academia isn't being used to its potential is a grotesque understatement. However, I would be irresponsible if I failed to emphasize again the incredibly hard work of writing faculty and English teachers, and everyone else across the curricular landscape who involves writing in their pedagogies. To give you a sense of what that might require, at one institution, my course load involved four first-year writing courses per semester, each with about thirty students, each student writing multiple papers and multiple drafts of those papers. Consider that even if all my students only submitted one five-page paper the entire semester, that's 600 pages of writing to read. But then consider that there were multiple drafts of multiple assignments, and I responded in writing to every single one. And then consider that some compositionists face even bigger workloads.

And too many first-year writing programs are understaffed in terms of full-time, fully trained professors; colleges farm out many courses to adjuncts, many of whom aren't really compositionists. Some adjuncts are great at what they do. But many lack requisite training. I've personally seen guidance counselors, math teachers, and people with master's degrees in philosophy or history hired to teach first-year writing. Upon hiring one lawyer as an adjunct writing instructor, one department chair said to me, "If that guy can write effective legal briefs given how precise those need to be, he clearly can handle this course." Well, no. That guy might have been an exceptional legal writer, but being a great writer doesn't mean he knows a lick about how to teach other people to write. That's why there's an entire discipline devoted exclusively to researching how to effectively teach writing. It's that complicated. And it's that important.

So, I end this chapter with a reminder that compositionists and everyone involving writing in their courses need more support, not more criticism. Writing holds great potential in the academy, and we should empower those who take on the extra labor of employing it.

NOTORIOUS JTG

I've shown that the pedagogies education employs—lecture, "active" learning, writing, etc.—broadly fail to foster critical thinking. But what if they not only fail to foster critical thinking, what if they actually suppress it?

Enter a favorite educational curmudgeon of mine, John Taylor Gatto, a.k.a. JTG, and his book, *Dumbing Us Down*. The book's first chapter, *The Seven-Lesson Schoolteacher*, succinctly excoriates modern American education for making it nearly impossible for students to become intellectually engaged, make meaning, and think critically. Gatto argues that academia's real lessons bear absolutely no relationship to subject matter or course content. In line with my point that *the pedagogy is the lesson*, Gatto argues that academia's real lessons are passivity and compliance to institutional power structures. And if you want to know why JTG is "notorious," it is because he first delivered the *The Seven-Lesson Schoolteacher's* academic excoriations to an auditorium of educators and administrators while accepting the New York state Teacher of the Year award.

I could write a book on each of Gatto's seven lessons, but I'll limit myself to these two:

> *Confusion: "Everything* I teach is out of context. I teach the un-relating of everything...I teach too much: the orbiting of planets, the law of large numbers, slavery, adjectives... choral singing...surprise guests, fire drills...computer languages...What do any of these things have to do with each other?"

Indifference: "I do it by demanding that they become totally involved in my lessons...But when the bell rings I insist they drop whatever it is we have been doing and proceed quickly to the next work."

Gatto and McLuhan ("the medium is the message") would have gotten along well, don't you think? Each in their own way realized that *how* we teach entirely eclipses what we teach. To elucidate *confusion* and *indifference* as two dominant lessons in academia, I offer this analogy:

I abduct you and your friends and drop you all in a junkyard, and I start telling you random things about the junk. From nine to ten, I tell you about the history of the junkyard. From ten to eleven, I tell you about the properties of some of the different junk, e.g., "these old tires used innertubes with rubber farmed from Indonesia." From eleven to twelve, we talk about the appliances we find. I also mention the upcoming test on junk facts! All the while, what your brain really wants to know is this: What the hell am I doing in this junkyard? What value does any of this have to my life? Why do I need to know any of this at all?

Now let me offer a different scenario: I drop you and your friends into the same junkyard and tell you that in three days the people from the junkyard down the road will try to kill you all. Suddenly— *instantaneously*—all the junk in the yard metamorphosizes. It's no longer junk. It's weaponry. And suddenly you possess immediate reasons and incentives for learning about the physical properties of the junk, the culture of the other junk tribe, the history of prior battles, etc.

Or, I tell you that in one week we will open the yard and sell whatever we can. Or, I tell you that we need medicine. Or, I tell you that winter is coming.

With purpose and context, your presence in the junkyard holds meaning. Without purpose and context, it doesn't. Unfortunately, student brains see most of what school offers as purposeless, random information-junk. Period one is information-junk about the Revolutionary War. Period two is information-junk from a book about some kids on an island fighting over a seashell. Period three is information-junk about the different kinds of lava. Period four is information-junk about what happens when we do things with numbers. Nothing learned in any of the periods has anything to do with anything learned from the other periods. And as much as we tell students that we want them to become deeply, passionately engaged in Shakespeare, we equally tell them that they must douse that Shakespearean passion the moment Pavlov's bell rings, at which moment they should instantly become just as passionate about chemical reactions. That disconnect between subjects is *confusing*, and the lack of connection between learning and their daily lives obviously makes them *indifferent*.

For student brains, the miscellany of school information makes about as much sense as this "taxonomy of the animal kingdom" discovered by Jorge Borges[68] and "attributed to an ancient Chinese encyclopedia entitled the *Celestial Emporium of Benevolent Knowledge*: On those remote pages it is written that animals are divided into (a) those that belong to the Emperor, (b) embalmed ones, (c) those that are trained, (d) suckling pigs, (e) mermaids, (f) fabulous ones, (g) stray dogs, (h) those that are included in this classification, (i) those that tremble as if they were mad, (j) innumerable ones, (k) those drawn with a very fine camel's hair brush, (l) others, (m) those that have just broken a flower vase, (n) those that resemble flies form a distance." If your mind struggles to make sense of that list, and I hope it does, then consider that it makes as much sense to you as does random information to student brains about the Civil War ("a good soldier could reload, aim, and fire a musket about three times a minute") followed forty-minutes later by information about elements ("NA is the periodic symbol for sodium.") Some tidbits of information might be interesting—I actually remember the musket information from my 7th grade history class (but I don't know if it is true or not)—and some might prove useful at some future point. But none of that matters here. What matters here is that to the *brain* of a child, *school information* is no different than the *Celestial Emporium of Benevolent Knowledge*.

But don't take my word for it. There's vast evidence that students don't retain information they supposedly "learn," even when they do well on tests. In fact, less-so, proportionately, when they do well on tests. Most studies show a very bleak picture. A more "favorable" study[69] that tracked recall or "persistence" after a final exam found that students who took the course, on average, devolved "halfway [back] to [the] control group score"—the score by students who never even took the course—just 13 weeks after the course. In other words, 13 weeks later, students forgot half of what they learned. Furthermore, A students, perhaps because they acquired more information-junk to forget, forgot at a faster rate than C students. The result was that A students retained barely more information-junk than C students two-years after the course. (Note, therefore, that in terms of what students will actually retain from a course two years later, *it makes more sense for them to just earn a C than strive for the A;* both groups will end up recalling similar amounts of information-junk regardless.)

Unfortunately, Gatto's *confusion* and *indifference* don't just prevent recall, they suppress curiosity. *The Hungry Mind, by Susan Engels,* describes how she found that while kindergarteners would average 2.36 "episodes of curiosity" every two hours, 5th graders only displayed .48 episodes every two hours, about an 80 percent decline.[70] Worse, she found that "nine of the ten [5th grade] classrooms had a least one two-hour stretch where there were no expressions of curiosity" at all. Rather than encouraging curiosity, school kills it. Like Notorious JTG said, school teaches students to be confused and indifferent.

5 PERCENT

That trend carries forward to higher education. In her book, *My Freshman Year: What a Professor Learned by Becoming A Student,* Rebekah Nathan, an anthropologist, found herself so baffled by her students' lackluster academic behavior that she enrolled as a student and lived in the residence halls for a year. Nathan found that "although there was occasional talk about academics, it accounted for less than 5 percent of the total subjects [she] heard discussed.... Virtually none of the talk, aside from out-of-class meetings for a group project or joint homework sessions, concerned either the substantive content of a class or any other topic that might be labeled academic or intellectual."

And there you have it. Students care so much about school curricula that it accounts for a whopping 5 percent of what they talk about outside of class. The rousing residence hall debates about the most feminist character in Shakespeare, about whether or not we should have invaded Iraq, the pressing implications of Greek philosophy on contemporary American thought, the impact of the bulbous bow invention for ships in terms global hegemony: those conversations never happen.

Likewise, it's challenging to recount even just a few times over 30 years in academia that I arrived at my own class to find students discussing the intellectual content from another class. More likely, if students discussed their other classes at all, they would discuss the upcoming test, or the test they just took, or the test they just got back, or whether or not they like the teacher, or just about anything *but* its intellectual content.

In fact, the notion students should actually feel invested in the subject matter of their classes has become so absurd that many no longer even consider it something that *should* happen. One of my favorite quotations that highlights this dates back to 1992.[71] Interviewed for a research study, the student said, "If you are under a lot of pressure then you will just concentrate on passing the course.... One subject I wasn't very good at I tried to understand the subject and I failed the exam. When I re-took the exam I just concentrated on passing the exam. I got 96 percent and the guy couldn't understand why I failed the first time. I told him this time I just concentrated on passing the exam rather than understanding the subject. I still don't understand the subject so it defeated the object, in a way." Studying to pass school, even though he didn't understand the material, *only* defeated the purpose of education *"in a way"!* Studying without learning *only* kinda-sorta undermined the student's conception of education. That student, and any who would make a similar remark about earning a grade without understanding the content, don't even consider that school actually should be intellectually engaging and improve their lives.

In contrast, I know that all educators will recount some students who they genuinely turned on to a given subject matter. To be *sure*, some students arrive at college with pre-existing passions for certain subjects, students who just love literature or feel a calling to become a nurse. And, to the credit of educators who find ways to make history or enzymatic reactions fascinating, some students get turned on to particular subjects during their educational experiences.

But none of that changes the broader and flawed construct that the Notorious JTG points out. Up and down the K-Ph.D. ladder, students might study the Industrial Revolution in history (where someone predetermined the number of "important" information bits) and then read *Huckleberry Finn* in English, and never the "twain" shall meet. Why do they need to learn about the aging refrigerators in the junkyard, I mean, the Industrial Revolution? Doesn't matter. What does Huck Finn have to do with the Industrial Revolution? Nothing. How does any of that help them on their next date? They don't know (and it doesn't).

Now contrast that experience against how we learn in life. From the moment infants start learning, they learn things that carry meaningfulness and value—how to get affection, how to point to the milk bottle, how to move around, etc. They don't learn facts about milk; they learn how to get it. In all of life, we learn by making sense of things—connecting them. We learn out of necessity *(meaningfulness rather than indifference)*, and we learn through connections *(relationships rather than confusion)*. All of that also inherently *demands* thinking.

For example, my parenting—everyone's parenting—emerges from the *confluence* of the things in my world rather than from disparateness. My parenting is a constantly evolving amalgamation of the history of parenting in this country, my economic status, my profession, the nature of my education, my core philosophies, my ability to cook ("Dad, I'm hungry."), how my parents parented, the friends with whom I keep company, what happens in politics, discoveries in science, what happens in my child's education, etc. In my life, in all our lives, and in everything we do, "different" subjects interact all the time, and in ways that matter. (And it's that interconnectedness of learning in life, by the way, that just prompted Finland, which typically achieves the highest educational outcomes in the world, to announce that it will do away with formal subject areas.). In life, we all use thinking to *connect* things in *meaningful* ways that improve our lives.

American education is predicated on the opposite, and the disciplinary disparateness hurts little brains. Remember the *basal ganglia*—the part of the brain that releases dopamine to give us pleasure? Well, it becomes active when we engage in tasks that involve "meaning making" but *not in tasks such as rote memorization.*[72] Therefore, it only makes sense that students talked about the intellectual content of their courses a meager 5 percent of the time when out of class. The student brain *should* be bored by *confusing information for which it has no use, and to which it is indifferent.* ("Come here, children, so I can regale you about the junkyard's wonderful collection of rusty compressor gaskets!")

Fortunately, the research doesn't just show us how education can bore students, it also shows us how it can engage them. Students actually *enjoy* assignments that prompt them to think. One of the larger studies found that "first-year and senior students who reported that more of their writing assignments required meaning-making were especially likely to report greater participation."[73] Long story short: meaning-making, as in writing to think, catalyzes student engagement. Students like it. Their brains evolved to want it.

Unfortunately, what Notorious JTG so aptly points out is that when education separates information from meaning, it causes students to become *confused* and *indifferent*. That kind of education isn't just non-meaningful, it's *dysmeaningful*—actively structured so as to thwart connection to other subjects, and more so to life itself. Somewhere along the line, we determined that *what* students learn matters most. We didn't pay enough attention to the fact that *it's the pedagogy that is the lesson.*

I can seldom raise this objection to subject-centered learning without educators, parents, or corporate leaders raising the "but-what-about-blank" objection, which is the argument that there are just certain bodies of factual information that people need to know. "But what about…" the founding of the United States, slavery, climate change, chemical reactions, Shakespeare, the Holocaust? Don't some things *need* to be learned? No!

No subject matters one lick if students lack the capacity to *think* about it. As important as the Revolutionary War might be, students don't need to learn about it in order to live better lives. Students do *need* critical thinking to live better lives.

That said, I'm *not* really arguing against subject matter or information. I'm talking about making thinking primary, and critical thinking always brings subject matter along for the ride. Students can only exercise critical thinking when there is a *something* to think about, so subjects are nice too (and subjects can be historical or scientific or literary or anything else), but we need to give primacy to thinking about information and meaningfully connecting it to life.

MAKING MEANING

Unfortunately, it's the information chase on which most education is still predicated. And that information chase is more gangrenous than you might think. It assaults education in surprising ways. Trying to serve students well by delivering information as clearly as possible, educators "write lesson plans that present information in sequential order," trying to make information as clear and as simple to understand as possible. This seems to make sense, right? The clear presentation of information must produce the best outcomes.

But consider what really happens: If educators present information so clearly that students don't even need to think about it, then students don't need to *think*...about it. And according to a good deal of research, the clear presentation of highly scaffolded information "may not take advantage of the brain's natural learning system."[74]

Taking advantage of that natural learning system means prodding the brain to think, which is why you might now appreciate why *clear lectures are less effective than confusing ones*. Note, however, that "confusing" here, as an *intentional* pedagogical device, is different from Gatto's use of "confusion," which refers to his contention that education is impossibly nonsensical to students. (If that point about confusing lectures strike you as wrong, you also might ask yourself if your own education indoctrinated you into thinking that the clear presentation of information is best.) What Steve Kolowich found was not only that the "students who had watched the more confusing videos learn more" but that "the students who watched the more straightforward videos learn, on average, nothing—even though they walked away thinking they had a better understanding of the material."[75]

Why do students learn nothing from the clearest lectures? Because the brain could not care less about memorizing bits of dysmeaningful information-junk. That bores it. It hurts. So, it shuts off. In contrast, the brain loves making meaning, which it evolved to do. That means that the brain likes to take something complex—such as a confusing lecture (or just about everything it encounters in life)—and connect the dots in a way that *makes sense to it*, not in ways that make sense to someone else. That's why "confusing students on purpose is...like loading the elastic of a slingshot: It creates tension that can propel [students] into higher altitudes of understanding. Pull too far, though, and the elastic will snap."[76]

Pull just right, though, and the opportunity to make meaning is a student's intellectual aphrodisiac. It plays on what Piaget termed, "cognitive disequilibrium", which is that when the brain finds something confusing, it will instinctively think about that thing until it resolves that confusion. Evolution programmed *homo sapiens* to do that; it's how we survived. But if the brain cannot make sense of the situation, or if there's just information to memorize—the Gatto kind of *confusion*—then evolution programmed our brains to disregard it. After all, why would a brain want to store information for which it sees no meaning, purpose, or immediate application in life? What use is information that doesn't improve our chances to survive?

We consider a "good student" to be the one who will persevere through JTG's *confusion* and *indifference*, who will pay attention at the junkyard. But is that really the student we want? When a "good student" does so and finds "a purpose for finding meaningless answers, the student is usually motivated by issues related to power or obedience such as pleasing someone else or getting a grade, or preparing for an exam."[77] That student performs school well for the rewards of school, but not because school is stimulating their critical thinking, nor because school is meaningful in their lives—it still won't help them on their next date. Yet despite the need to help students make meaning of *their* own, "well-intentioned educators often assume that their [own] questions are the best ones, and the ones that matter to students," but the best question is always the one "the student cares about,"[78] never the one from the teacher.

IS IT GOING TO BE ON THE TEST?

Given the construct I've described, can you guess the single question that students care about most? It's "Is this going to be on the test?" Educators hate this question and denounce its inquisitors for their inability to see the inherent gilded nobility of learning for learning's sake. These educators, passionate as they are about the junkyard's collection of pre-WWII road signs, are filled with righteous indignation that the students don't see why pre-WWII road signs are important.

But *"Is this going to be on the test?" is the single most sensible question any student can ask.* If information lacks immediate value in the student's actual life—if its value only emerges *if and when* it appears on a test—then what kind of idiot wouldn't ask that question? That's the *only relevant* question. So don't blame the students; credit them.

We are the ones who set up the game.

We created an educational system built on *confusion* and *indifference*.

The students are playing by *our* rules: Rule number one is that what matters is only what is tested. Rule number two is that good test scores matter. And there's no rule number three.

But I want to make sure the real problem is clear. The problem is not that students *don't* want their education to help them *think* about meaningful things; the problem is that academia (typically) makes it *impossible* for them to do so. So, they learn early on, before they're even semi-aware of it, perhaps from the very first gold star in kindergarten, certainly by around the end of primary school, to stop expecting learning to be meaningful. By the time they graduate high school, they've spent twelve years learning that school *doesn't* help them on their next date, and then college faculty are nevertheless surprised that students don't just love *learning*?

But they don't. When asked for the "main reasons [they] chose to attend university," about 35 percent responded that they wanted a good job and about 28 percent wanted a specific career, but less than 10 percent wanted "an education or [to] better themselves"[79] intellectually. Students don't discuss the intellectual substance of classes, and they don't attend college to better themselves. They are confused and indifferent, and, given that college has failed to help them date, they should be.

I'll leave this chapter with these words from Frank Breslin.[80] He says it better than me.

> *What better way to frustrate the burning idealism of youth intent on bettering their lives through higher education than by burdening them with crippling debt and sidelining them in securing an education that might later challenge the status quo.*

Better to prevent future protests from even occurring by wearing down students in their middle-school years with the soul-numbing drudgery of standardized testing that cools their ardor about coming to school, let alone about going to college.

Better to smother their desire for learning by an eternal night of rigged testing lest the excitement of critical thinking prove contagious and challenges policies of social injustice against a government that wages economic warfare against its own people.

Imagine students conditioned by years of these tests that attempt to brainwash them into thinking that every question must have a right answer; trained to accept the framework they're given rather than thinking outside it and resist the indoctrination of believing whatever they're taught.

Imagine the effect on students of being deprived not only of critical thinking, but also of learning even one viewpoint because the curriculum that would have prepared them for high school is no longer taught— traditional subjects such as science, history, literature, world languages, art, and music—because all they're now doing is preparing for tests.

ANGLES OF ENTRY

"The corrections officer cued up a short clip on his computer monitor that showed two men standing across from each other... they were practicing stabbing techniques.... It looked like a stabbing motion, but it was slow and methodical, from strange angles that didn't seem like they would be very effective.

This was not a typical approach to stabbing someone—it wasn't like anything I learned in hand-to-hand combat training in the military, or that I'd seen in any of the hundreds of other prison videos I've watched. The prisoner mimicking an attack wasn't targeting the spleen, liver, neck, or even the upper chest area where people are typically trained to strike with a knife. He was stabbing different areas of the torso, at different angles of entry."
—Larkin's, *When Violence is the Answer*

What's interesting and terrifying about Tim's account is what motivated the inmates to stab in such odd ways. And what motivated the inmates' odd movements was what happened the day before. And what happened the day before was that the corrections officers broke up a fight in the yard. Why was there a fight in the yard? Because the inmates staged it. They staged it because the guards got new body armor, which meant that inmates needed to sneak a peak at the new armor's openings. The unconventional stabbing motions were practice for shanking the guards at the precise angles where the new armor was flawed.

Normally, the fact that the officers broke up the fight would make it appear as though the officers were the ones in control. But, in reality, the inmates, who staged the fight, were controlling the guards.

Though schools are *not* prisons, students nevertheless also always look for their own "different angles of entry." They look to control the system. And why shouldn't they? Faced with an education of *confusion* and *indifference*, an education not centered on thinking and meaning making, an education of accumulating information-junk, and an education where the most visible reward is a grade, it only makes sense that students would look to control the situation in order to get to those good grades.

This is sad and beautiful at the same time: It's sad because students should use their thinking skills for more noble and educational reasons than figuring out how to beat the system. But it is *beautiful* because students, good *homo sapiens* that they are, will always find ways to think critically, even if it is through efforts to control the very educational structure that's otherwise suppressing them from thinking in the first place.

Here's an example of a student-staged fight in the yard: It's the fourth week of the semester and as you start class, it becomes apparent that most of the students didn't do the assigned reading.

(Assigned reading is something many students naturally resist. They resist it because it's typically reading students would never do if they were to pick up a book of their choosing, a book *they* find interesting, a book relevant to *their* lives. If students can't "make meaningful connections with text," then the real "goal and purpose of reading is completely lost."[81] With the meaningful purpose lost, students rightly resist assigned readings.)

Regardless of why they didn't do the reading, you still face a dilemma: You need to keep on schedule and cover all the course material. If you don't, students won't pass the standardized test toward the end of the year and/or they will not exit your class prepared for the next class in the sequence. Or, even if there is no standardized test, if you just press on and students do poorly, what happens to your teaching evaluations? Or, what happens if the administration sees your test scores plummet? What happens if half your students fail every semester? What does that say about *you* as a teacher?

Facing very real repercussions for high failure rates, you decide that rather than sending your students back to do the reading, or just letting them fail, you give your students a (perfectly well-organized and exceptionally clear, not-at-all-confusing) lecture that explains the reading in its entirety. (Note: *Any* reading that can be explained more easily through lecture is a reading that students probably don't really need to do anyway. Students know this. Reading just to acquire information is fine, but lecture can do that more easily for students, and students prefer lectures because lectures require less effort than reading. Reading for meaning making, on the other hand, can never be supplanted by lecture.)

Returning to the point, what really happened when the students refused to do the assigned reading was that they staged a fight in the yard to get a look at the flaws in your armor. They observed how you reacted. And, since *pedagogy is the lesson*, what you taught them by lecturing to compensate for their laziness is that, more than anything else, they *never* need to do the reading again. You taught them that you'll lecture in order to make up for the work they don't do. You also just proved what they suspected all along: Reading really isn't important anyway. If it were, you would make them do it. The only thing that really matters (for them *and* for you) is doing well on the test, and the information for doing so is nothing more than a means to that end.

I can't count the number of times educators have confided in me about falling into this trap. "What else can I do?" they ask. "The students need the information...to pass the course...to learn this material...to be prepared for the next course...to pass the state boards...etc." To ensure that assigned-reading arduousness gets done, educators either lecture the information or enact increasingly draconian penalties for not reading, such as reading quizzes or weekly tests. But doing so only pours gasoline on the fire; it only makes students want to beat the system all the more. And why shouldn't it? Who wants to feel coerced into reading about the junkyard's amazing collection of peel-top tin cans?

But though a real problem, the reading problem is actually the red herring. What matters is *why* students challenge the system in the first place. What is their desire to resist telling us? "Too often," Tolman, Sechler, and Smart write in *Why Students Resist Learning,* "instructors react to manifestations of resistance as though they are noise, background static, that disrupts the 'communication' signal the faculty member is trying to get across, usually content…this purported 'noise' is often responded to with frustration and a desire to just bypass it and move on to the 'important stuff.' However, what if the resistance is the important stuff?"

It *is* the important stuff. We need to realize that students are not only *confused* by and *indifferent* about school. We need to realize that they *resist* it. And the resistance is the *signal.* And how are those critical-thinking *homo sapiens* doing with respect to their efforts to control the system? They're *winning.*

Students are so effective at resisting that academia is bending to their resistance, and "if a culture of entitlement reigns among students in such a way that they reject the standards of achievement set by the academic community and if the academic community bends to the pressure of the culture of entitlement, then the integrity of the academic process is lost; and both the entitled and the gatekeepers of achievement lose. University degrees [and *all* degrees] become meaningless to the givers and the receivers."[82] In other words, if the students can manipulate the game such that their educators also don't care about meaningful intellectual development, then they can get the grades they need without working for them.

Which brings us to grade inflation. Student resistance is a "powerful factor fueling grade inflation,"[83] and if you don't think grade inflation is real, know that the percentage of students earning an A increased 28 percent between 1960 and 2009.[84] But that might be conservative. At Florida State University, the percentage of students earning an A in oceanography rose from 19 percent to 57 percent in just ten years.[85] Another study on California schools, which actually offered a morsel of hope that grade inflation might soon level off (but not decline), determined that *"all* [of the universities studied had] grade distributions that are high overall" even though some did not meet the standards for statistically significant grade inflation.[86] But half of them did. Most showed an upward trend, whether statistically significant or not. Oh, and 47 percent of high school seniors graduated with an A average in 2016, up from 38 percent in 1998—so basically half of all students are A students.[87]

But isn't it possible that increased grades actually represent more learning? Isn't it possible that improved teaching methods have resulted in greater percentages of students attaining higher outcomes? Nope. Not when the College Board[88] found that despite the rising GPAs, SAT scores are actually *falling*. In roughly the same period that grades inflated, the average SAT score fell from 1,026 to 1,002.[89]

Worse, research actually reveals that grade inflation undermines learning; it shows that stricter grading, not inflated grading, results in stronger test scores.[90] The reason isn't exactly mysterious. As one student put it, "If I get the same grade for my very best work that I get for work that is not my very best, I'm less motivated to try to stretch as far as I can."[91] Of *course,* grade inflation makes students less motivated. Smart *Homo sapiens* always try to figure out the easiest way to the highest reward. (Ultimately, we don't want students just chasing grades. As I will discuss in Section II, internal or intrinsic motivation is the real goal. But merely lowering grading standards doesn't increase intrinsic motivation. Doing so requires the pedagogies I'll discuss later.)

But grade inflation also corrupts student motivation to "stretch" in other unseen ways. One such way is that there's a critical difference between *individual* and *class-wide* grade expectations: *Individually* speaking, the isolated "student who expects an A…studies about 10 minutes less"[92] than the isolated student in the same class "who expects the B." That individual student who expects the A, perhaps confident in his or her own ability, proportionally scales his or her effort to the class's ability.

But the amount of effort students invest changes far more

dramatically when they *collectively* expect high grades, i.e., when the entire class knows that the *teacher* is an easy A. A "class filled with students who expect an A…features an average study time more than *50 minutes lower*" than a class that expects a B. Thus, the confident individual student might study ten minutes less, but *all* of the students will study *50 minutes less* when they know the teacher grades easily.

Again, in that construct—the one we set up—the students are *not* lazy for trying to do less; they're doing the most thoughtful thing any *homo sapiens* would do for survival in any environment—using their thinking skills to reason their way to the easiest path for the highest reward. Why expend unnecessary effort? Why put in time you don't need? Why put in more time than your peers? Why try to learn if everyone else is going to get an A regardless of whether they really learn the material or not?

Some educators certainly push back against the inclination to inflate grades, but even those who try to might not successfully hold the line. Grade inflation has become so perniciously pervasive that faculty do not even know the distribution of grades they're assigning. In one study, "nearly all of the interviewed professors believed their grades were lower than they actually were" to such an extent that even though faculty estimated a distribution of 11 percent As and 24 percent Bs, the distribution was actually 62 percent As and 33 percent Bs. That distribution, by the way, leaves *only 5 percent of the remaining scores available for all of the Cs, Ds, and Fs combined.*

Through generations of staging fights in the yard such as not doing the reading, students have bent the academic universe to their goals so successfully that about one-third of students believe they deserve a "B" for just attending regularly, and about 40 percent believe the same just for doing reading assignments.[93] Students make clear allusions to how they should automatically earn good grades as a result of how much they pay, because professors "work for" them— the students.[94]

In fact, education continues to embolden students such that tacit forms of resistance have turned direct and confrontational.

Faculty members report students standing in their office, declaring "I'm not leaving your office until you change my grade to an A!"[95] Other studies show students with higher attitudes of entitlement who "expected to surf the internet for fun and text message during class without repercussion…expected prompt responses to voice and email [and] were most likely to take offense when appointments are cancelled."[96] Resistance like this is most likely to come from white males from affluent households,[97] but if we're going to start finger pointing, we can't leave out parents who complete homework assignments for their kids[98] or who reward good grades with money or gifts, which further fosters entitlement[99] (which sends the message that education is good for the *other things* it gets you, such as money, rather than for its inherent value).

Yet, in higher education, students possess a far more powerful means of resistance and control than just an office tirade, and that tool for resistance is course evaluations. Research offers no complete resolution as to the extent that students use course evaluations to diminish rigor, but the evidence certainly suggests at least some "tit for tat".[100] For example, students who just failed an exam rate educators lower than students who passed the exam. Professors know this and therefore think they "can 'buy' better evaluation scores by inflating students' grade expectations."[101]

There are other factors in course evaluations but, in a nutshell, they amount to a "prisoner's dilemma" that one researcher called a "glaring illustration of Goodhart's Law."[102] Named for Charles Goodhart, Goodhart's Law means that "when a measure becomes a target, it ceases to be a good measure."[103] *No Child Left Behind* demonstrated Goodhart's Law terrifyingly well: The "measure" in question was standardized test scores. Hence, those scores stopped being an effective measure of learning. *All* that mattered was that the scores went up, not whether or not the students learned more deeply, and not whether or not the learning held value.

And doesn't Goodhart's Law play out perfectly in course evaluations? Professors, facing the need for strong student evaluations, especially if they need tenure, teach in ways that keep evaluations high: not too rigorous, some good song and dance, perhaps an extra credit assignment here or there, *lecturing about the reading to compensate for the fact that students didn't do it,* etc. It's not hard to understand why Derek Bruff calls this a "mutual nonaggression pact"[104] between faculty and students: The professor doesn't bust students' balls or ovaries too much. The students do some work. Everyone goes through the required motions. The students earn good grades. And students reciprocate with at-least-benign-or-better course evaluations.

Student evaluations can and should serve as one important measure of teaching. To make them more valuable, some theorists call for student evaluations that do better jobs of factoring workload, grade distribution, and other factors. Those calls unquestionably point in the right direction. *The inclusion of authentic standards for critical thinking as a way to measure learning outcomes between one course and the next would also serve an essential purpose in evaluating faculty; it would enable us to understand if better evaluations really equated with better outcomes. In other words, regardless of content acquisition, could the students think?*

Nevertheless, no one should find this present problem with evaluations surprising. It was we who built education as a transactional endeavor. It was we who designed school so as *not* to offer meaningful learning for *homo sapiens*. It was we who put the emphasis on the grades. It was we who created classes where brains are bored. Since school doesn't help students "on their next date" and since students can't not-go to school, they play the game for the rewards it offers and work the system as much as possible to get the only thing that matters: the grade.

> *Here—take my money. Now cheat me. Give me*
> *the least quality for my money.*[105]
> –G. Jack Gravlee, speaking about students' attitudes

TECHADEMIA*

I preface this chapter that excoriates online and electronic learning by noting that I'm no luddite. Occasionally, in isolated contexts, online learning serves important functions. For example, I developed online learning on important social issues, such as sexual assault, binge drinking, and prescription drug abuse. Campuses, which faced (and still face) epidemics on those issues, were not equipped with the personnel to educate students about them *en masse*. And for some of those issues, online learning could do what in-person couldn't, such as allow sexual assault survivors to engage the content privately, and bring authentic testimonies from real survivors or recovering addicts to the students.

In a similar arena, because online learning can fill certain gaps, Dave and I have created online learning opportunities for schools, home schoolers, and parents around critical thinking. Many educators don't know how to explicitly teach critical thinking, and most parents have absolutely no idea how to approach the topic. And how could they? So, in certain contexts, online learning can do important work.

But it's just not a replacement for extended face-to-face interaction with sound pedagogy. As much as students do learn critical thinking online through our programming, Dave and I would do much more for them if they took an in-person course with us. The four-semester

---

* A crucial note for the COVID era. Whatever critiques I make here of online learning, none of it matters relative to the health and safety of the students, teachers, and everyone else. In other words, in times of a pandemic, let's celebrate online learning for what it can do to keep us safe rather than what it cannot do educationally. That said, given the extensive amount of online learning that has occurred, it is worth noting how educators and parents alike have so broadly come to realize that there is no complete substitute for in-person learning.

critical thinking cohort program we developed, for example, resulted in sophomores writing essays that would rival the work of graduate students.

Yet, even though face-to-face learning remains eminent, academia still pushes technological "solutions." For all its lethargy with respect to other meaningful pedagogical changes (remember: "initiatives inspired by academic literature are rare"), academia is quick to adopt "smart" classrooms, online learning communities, learning management software, tablets, etc. And with some pragmatic reason: technology makes parents think that schools are cutting edge. So, it can prove difficult, perhaps even financially perilous, to be that school that doesn't have classrooms full of technological whizziwangs.

But, broadly speaking, is technology improving critical thinking outcomes? (You know the answer.)

As we enter this discussion, know that there's a difference between *online learning*, which happens at a distance from the classroom and necessitates the use of an electronic device, and *electronic learning*, which involves the use of electronics in the classroom, such as reading via a tablet rather than a textbook. These two different types of tech-based learning overlap, but I'm going to deal with online learning first.

ONLINE LEARNING

Online learning is popular. One study showed that about 1.6 million students took at least one course online in 2002. In 2011, that figure rose to 6.6 million, about a 320 percent change.[106] The same study found that in 2002 "less than one-half of all higher education institutions reported online education was critical to their long-term strategy," but by 2012 that figure rose to about 70 percent. By 2017, over one-third of all U.S. college students reported taking at least one online course per semester.[107]

However, before I speak to the dark side of online learning, I want to note one of its arguable perks, which is that it certainly does create a pathway for many people who otherwise might not be able to attend courses in person to attain an education. Online learning grants the single parent, or the person in the remote location, or the parent who can only find time for schoolwork late at night, the means to attain a degree and improve their economic status. And that's *important*.

And at first glance, online and in-person learning seem to produce comparable outcomes. In 2003, "57.2 percent of academic leaders rated the learning outcomes in online education as the same or superior to those in face-to-face" education. In 2012, the figure rose to 77 percent.[108] In fact, in terms of what many educators *feel* about online learning, it "transports the student to a new cognitive environment which motivates and actives the students... [and] promotes active engagement...[and] improved academic achievement."[109] That *sounds* great.

Unfortunately, research doesn't support that perception. For example, some research has shown improved outcomes through online learning, but not when we drill down into the details. Steven Stack's[110] review of the research concluded that when online courses do show higher outcomes, students tend to be older, married, self-selected, and more likely to have taken previous courses. When we control for those differences, online learning isn't really better. Another study found that even though online learning seemed to produce "stronger" outcomes, there was "little to no difference in grade-based student performance between" online versus in-person courses once the research controlled for the caliber of the students prior to the online course.[111]

But even if outcomes seem comparable, the fact is that when learning online, students cheat *more*. In fact, one of the most recent studies found that students working online self-reported a four-times greater likelihood to cheat.[112] Faculty often lament that fact, and they frequently discuss how difficult it is to know who is even taking the test or writing the paper on the other end of the digital divide.

Cheating aside, one of the largest studies, which reviewed over 50,000 courses, found that students learning online are "8.4 percentage points less likely to complete [the course], 14.5 percentage points less likely to pass…[and] 11.0 percentage points less likely to receive an A or B."[113]

Yet, none of the factors above touch the crux of the issue, which is that most research comparisons assess the effectiveness of online learning against the same traditional course structures this book has critiqued thus far. So, yes, students might pass the multiple-choice test or write the summary of other people's ideas as effectively online as in person, but a parity in achieving misguided goals isn't anything to laud.

So, what happens when we pit online learning against learning that isn't about information but about the development of meaningful skills such as critical thinking? There's not a tremendous amount of research on this question, but the research that does exist paints a grim picture. For example, one study examined whether or not students could learn equivalent negotiation *skills* (rather than just information about how to negotiate) when doing so online versus in person. Not surprisingly, they found that "face-to-face learners earned higher negotiation outcomes than online learners *even when using the same technology*,"[114] meaning that even when the in-person learners used computers to interact in the classroom, their physical proximity to the other human beings actually enhanced how much they learned. Physical presence matters.

Other efforts to achieve deeper learning and greater student engagement online run into significant pitfalls. For example, much online student-student interaction, and student-teacher interaction, occurs through discussion boards in which students "asynchronously" post different comments at different times rather than having an actual discussion.[115] They are similar to the postings you might see on Facebook, where different people post different things at different times in response to different posts. Such a medium imperils contiguous thought, which is why a study that compared class-based problem solving to online problem solving found that "computer-mediated communication resulted in significantly *longer* time-on-task for the same learning outcomes as the [face-to-face] group. The [computer] group spent approximately 23 percent more time-on-task than the [face-to-face] groups. It would have been appropriate had the finding been associated with superior outcomes,"[116] but the online students achieved less. The researchers called it "a matter for concern." Indeed.

The examples go on and on, but Jakub Grygiel captures it best when he writes that online learning misses the real "purpose of education," which is really supposed to "transcend whatever we happen to be learning at the moment." True education "shapes young personalities in their advancement toward a mature social life. It also teaches students how to become teachers themselves, something most of us will do in our own lives, if only as a parent." However, "by replacing real people with a 'virtual community' we are creating social deserts. As a society, do we really want to encourage the development of solitary pseudo-Protean individuals? Just as pornography is not a good preparation for marriage, so online education, shorn of interpersonal encounters, is a poor preparation for society."[117]

ELECTRONIC LEARNING

Some other troubling aspects of online learning come from the inherently problematic nature of electronic media (online or not). Sure, 79 percent of students report that learning through electronic devices is more fun,[118] but "fun", as I'll talk about much more in Section II, has *nothing* to do with effective education. (Education should be engaging, motivating, and interesting, yes. But "fun" isn't necessary, and potentially distracting.)

Fun is nevertheless what students will seek, especially when their brains can't make meaning through their education. And technology can become their escape from that deeper frustration with dysmeaningful learning. For example, when students use laptops in classes, they spend roughly 40 percent of class time on entirely non-academic purposes such as checking social media, watching videos, and playing games.[119] Not surprisingly, that leads to poorer academic performance. In fact, researchers "found that nonacademic internet use was frequently observed and was inversely related to performance on the cumulative final exam. This relationship was observed regardless of interest in the class, motivation to succeed, and intelligence. Moreover, accessing the Internet *for academic purposes* during class was not related to a benefit in performance."[120] Put succinctly, laptops in class diminish learning.

And when I speak about students' usage of electronic devices, please don't think I'm exclusively referencing computers. Or even tablets. To the contrary, 83 percent of students report using their phones for at least one course activity, and 25 percent report using their phones for *all* their courses at one point.[121] I have had students who typed entire papers on their phones. That never works out well.

Putting aside the ridiculousness of attempting to write a paper on a phone, the very medium of screens is problematic in itself. Without even looking at the damaging effects of screen time for younger children (who should never be allowed on screens, period), multiple studies[122,123,124] on young people of different ages support that internet/gaming "addiction" or high-volume usage connects to the atrophy of gray matter areas in the frontal lobe (including the pre-frontal cortex), which is responsible for executive functions around planning, governing impulses, and seeing tasks through. It also creates troublingly "spotty" white matter. But white matter matters a lot; it enables communication between the different regions of the brain, which means we need to help students build more of it rather than less. Screen time not only diminishes white matter, it also negatively impacts the brain's capacity for empathy and the processing of physical signals tied to emotion. And don't even get me started on what screen time is doing to attention spans (which is *not* a call to cater to shorter attention spans but rather a mandate to help our students lengthen them again).

There's more research on screen time than I can discuss here, and all of it reeks. But I do want to focus on an issue of particular importance to academia: *reading*. There's formidable effort in academia to move away from paper texts. Partially, this stems from a noble desire to save students money on what are often ridiculously expensive textbooks. Other motivations range from wanting to save students the trouble of schlepping heavy books (as if that exercise would be bad), to thinking that students enjoy reading on screens more, to actually wanting to supplant reading with multimedia stimulation through videos and games (because maybe we can distract students from the fact that learning isn't meaningful by making it fun).

Unfortunately, even though it might seem as though reading is the same whether it occurs on screen or off, the different mediums hardly compare. The totality of *why* the brains read differently on screens isn't fully known yet, but some of it has to do with the lack of physicality of electronically generated words; as ephemeral as it sounds, something about the "thereness" of books and physical texts makes a difference.[125]

One recent study[126] compared kids who read versus kids who spent more time on screen. It found that while "time spent reading [offline] was positively correlated with higher functional connectivity between the seed area and left-sided language, visual and cognitive control regions," more "screen time was related to lower connectivity between the seed area and regions related to language and cognitive control." Since that's highly technical jargon, here's the nutshell:

Reading builds better brain connections.

Screen time doesn't.

Perhaps no researcher offers more on this topic than Maryanne Wolf. For a quick glance at what she has to say, read her article *Skim Reading is the New Normal: The Effect on Society is Profound*. For a deeper look, I recommend her book, *Reader Come Home: The Reading Brain in a Digital World*. Here are just a few key findings out of many:

(From the article)

- High school students "who read on print were superior in their comprehension to screen-reading peers, particularly in their ability to sequence detail and reconstruct the plot in chronological order."
- "critical analysis, empathy, and other deep reading processes" suffer when reading digitally and might become "'collateral damage' of our digital culture"

(From the book)

- 5th graders preferred reading on screen but achieved better comprehension in print
- A research study found that reading an e-book that kept students' attention through "bells and whistles" "often distracted beginning readers from the story narrative" and "were not helpful to building stronger reading skills."

The emerging picture, therefore, is simply that reading on a screen builds a different brain, and a worse one. We cannot persist under notions that screens and technology serve us as different but equal media, and we certainly cannot persist under the even-more-harmful fallacy that technology improves education overall.

POWERPOINT

Rounding out my tirade against technology, one of the larger electronic problems that persists in academic classrooms is PowerPoint (and its variants), which is still ubiquitous in college classrooms and increasingly present in K-12. If you want a more complete sense of PowerPoint's failings, you can find it on *Infusing PowerPoint with Critical Thinking*, an episode from *The Critical Thinking Initiative* podcast. But here's the skinny:

Foremost, "there is little consistent evidence...to show that teaching with PowerPoint leads to significantly better learning and significantly better grades.... A majority of studies shows that use of PowerPoint is not associated with a significant improvement in student grades."[127] At best, PowerPoint might be a null-tool when it comes to advancing education.

But educators nevertheless see it as "the Viagra of the spoken word...a wonder pill for flabby lectures,"[128] and hold the belief that cool technologies (and PowerPoint was at least once considered cutting edge) make for better learning. Therefore, it's still used a great deal, and I need to *mea culpa* that I use it sometimes as well, and that, as an *occasional* tool for specific purposes, such as presenting a truly *visual* aid, it can prove valuable.

Unfortunately, it also comes at great costs. PowerPoint forces lessons into linear, sequential, snippet-able presentations, which generally favor information over ideas. Ideas, on the other hand, can and often should be messy and nonlinear. As Brigadier General H. R. McMaster said, PowerPoint "is dangerous because it can create the illusion of understanding and the illusion of control. Some problems in the world are not bullet-izable."[129]

Furthermore, PowerPoint creates a non-interactive class structure where the educator presents information *to* the class rather than encouraging a more dynamic exchange, which returns us to many of the sins I discussed about lecture. And the fact that PowerPoint enables some fancy screen-things to occur during a lecture doesn't change *any* of lecture's fundamental flaws. In fact, even if we "assume (falsely) that PowerPoint is the greatest teaching tool since the invention of chalk," it still functions such that "most classroom teachers dim or shut off the classroom lights...[so] how can we expect our students to perform at their peak when we create a classroom environment that is conducive to sleeping?"[130]

Fundamentally, PowerPoint as a medium is not designed to get people *thinking*, but rather to get them watching, learning, absorbing, note taking, etc. *What we must ask of any teaching tool, foremost, is not whether or not it empowers the educator but whether or not it empowers the student.* PowerPoint helps teachers present, but it is an obstacle to cultivating in students the capacity to think, create, solve, invent, reason, speculate, etc.

SHORTING OUT

Technology not only typically fails to improve learning, in certain regards it undoubtedly hinders it, and it hurts the learner. As I'll talk about in the next section, learning is ultimately a fundamentally human endeavor best accomplished by humans actually interacting with other humans.

Therefore, we need to challenge academia's race to more and more technology. It's no fix for what's ailing education, but it is often treated as such. I could not recount to you the number of educational institutions or philanthropists who scoff when Dave and I suggest that they invest in faculty development around critical thinking, but who laud the number of tablets they just put in students' hands. Consider, for example, that in 2016, spending for educational technology in the U.S. for higher education and K-12 exceeded $10 *billion.* As educators fight for reasonable wages, as students struggle with reading, as learning outcomes suffer; as critical thinking wanes, the U.S. spends *billions* every year on "smart" classrooms, tablets, computers, and their ilk, none of which produce better critical thinkers or better *homo sapiens. Meanwhile, making students smart costs a slight fraction of what it costs to make classrooms "smart."* Teacher training is relatively cheap. Pedagogy costs nothing.

And the pedagogy is the lesson.

CONCLUSION TO SECTION I:
LET IT BURN

A perpetual theme I asserted thus far is that humans, students included, evolved to think critically, to solve problems, and to develop ideas. The brain rewards critical thinking, and the brain suffers when deprived of it. Therefore, at some point in their education, students tacitly or consciously use their innate thinking skills to question the flawed educational structure in which they are engulfed. At some point, their brains ask education to prove that it's making their brains better. And that's a beautiful thing. It shows us the human mind doing that thing no other creature can do: thinking.

How does our educational paradigm hold up to their scrutiny? It answers that it does not know how to teach them to think critically, leaving their "ability to reason about the information on the Internet" as *"bleak,"* and leaving them ranked eighteenth out of nineteen countries in "problem solving in a technology rich environment." It answers that direct instruction "hurts" and might actually "damage [their] brains." It answers by telling them, even at the college level, to spend most of their writing efforts, two-thirds of it, summarizing thoughts other people got to think rather than developing thoughts of their own. It answers that most educators believe they foster active learning environments even when the vast majority of students don't feel active. It answers in ways that are *confusing* and that leave students *indifferent* because what students really want is for education to help them on their next date. But it doesn't do that.

Is it really hard to fathom then that my classmates shouted along with Rock Master Scott? They'd already staged so many other fights in the yard. Why not one more?

In advising other generals what to do with their armies when confronted with near certain defeat, the great Chinese military strategist, Tu Yu, advised the following: "burn your baggage and impedimenta, throw away your stores and provisions, choke up the wells, destroy your cooking stoves, and make it plain to your men that they cannot survive but must fight to the death."[131] And *that* is why we should, metaphorically of course, burn down existing structures of education. We burn it not out of anger but because existing structures, e.g., direct instruction, are the "baggage and impedimenta...and cooking stoves" that make us believe we can survive this fight if we do not change, and change drastically.

My classmates didn't want all education turned to ash; they only wanted Section I's educational paradigm burnt down. They wanted education to light a fire, a fire in *them*. They wanted Yeats's education.

Now let's talk about how we can do that.

SECTION II

Yeats's Fire

*It is the thesis of this book that change—constant, accelerating, ubiquitous—
is the most striking characteristic of the world we live in and that our
educational system has not yet recognized this fact. We maintain, further,
that the abilities and attitudes required to deal adequately with change
are those of the highest priority and that it is not beyond our ingenuity to
design school environments which can help young people to master concepts
necessary to survival in a rapidly changing world. The institution we call
"school" is what it is because we made it that way...if, in short, it is not
doing what needs to be done, it can be changed; it must be changed.*
–Neil Postman & Charles Weingartner

Teaching as a Subversive Activity:
*A no-holds-barred assault on outdated teaching methods—with dramatic and
practical proposals on how education can be made relevant to today's world.*
–1969

INTRODUCTION TO SECTION II

I hope the journey through Section I wasn't *too* demoralizing, but I hope it helped explain my high school cohort's passion for Rock Master Scott & The Dynamic Three. Regardless, this half of the book will prove that education doesn't have to be *anything* like what it is now. It *can* foster critical thinking. It *can* be meaningful. It *can* make students passionate about learning.

But I need to qualify Section II in two very important ways:

QUALIFICATION ONE: TEACHING IS AN ART

We unequivocally need to apply educational science to education— something that happens far, far too little—but I want to make it clear that teaching is *not* just a science.

Teachers work in a dynamic medium—rooms filled with students of different subcultures, preparedness, personalities, intentions, desires, upbringings, genders, etc. Teachers only become successful when that heterogony of students collectively grows cognitively, socially, emotionally, psychologically, physically, etc. They must grow in *all their rich humanity*, and that makes the teaching of humans by humans the most complicated of all endeavors.

> *After some 30 years…I have concluded that classroom*
> *teaching is perhaps the most complex, most challenging,*
> *and most demanding, subtle, nuanced, and frightening*
> *activity that our species has EVER invented.*
> –Lee Shulman

Other research supports Shulman's point. In fact, one of the more comprehensive studies done, which studied students over 10 years at Hamilton College, found that what makes a college successful has nothing to do with the caliber faculty publications, nor its technology, nor its dormitories, but simply its *people* and the quality of the relationships between them, especially between student and teacher.[132]

Unfortunately, even though research can inform us about what pedagogies work better for teach*ing*, research doesn't offer us all too much when it comes to who makes a good teach*er*. As with all artists, the qualities that make for effective teachers remain remarkably ineffable.

If we look at some of the research around what makes for an effective teach*er*, and there really isn't very much relative to other educational topics, the outcomes offer us very little substance. One study[133] found that students (college and older) rated the top five qualities of an effective teacher as:

1. Love for the children
2. Love for the profession
3. Patience
4. Friendly attitude to the students
5. Equal attitude to all students

You might note that nothing in that list actually has anything to do with teaching effectively, not in the direct sense. Loving one's students or loving the profession or having patience or being friendly or treating people equally are all important, but not one of them necessarily produces learning outcomes. I have seen many a loving, patient educator who couldn't teach a lick. You have probably experienced such an educator as well.

The same study found that *teachers* ranked the most important qualities of a teacher as follows:

1. Love for the children
2. Love for the profession
3. Skillful teaching
4. Patience
5. Ability to involve the students in the work

That's as useless a list as the one that preceded it. It's not that love for one's students isn't important. It's assuredly important. It's just that loving one's students isn't the same as transforming them. Furthermore, ranking "skillful teaching" as third on the list of what makes for an effective teacher is curious since it would seem to *beg the answer*. Answering what makes a "good" teacher by saying "skillful teaching" is like answering what makes a good chef by saying "skillful cooking."

But that's the point. Teaching is an *art* so hard to define that another study ended up with no less than 102 student-generated traits that included everything from "being a good story teller" to good "grooming."[134]

As problematic as the research on an effective teach*er* is, I'm not against any of it. Nor do I oppose the vague lists. But no list will ever find the formula for a good teacher, much in the same way no one will ever be able to identify that "it" quality of a star actor.

Consider how, as I mentioned in Section I, one of the factors that makes "active learning" work is whether or not the teacher models traits such as intellectual curiosity and humility. How does one do that exactly? How often? When? What's the Goldie-Locks amount of intellectual curiosity versus expertise to exhibit?

Consider that, when it comes to whether or not students read, much less act on, feedback they receive on their papers, one of the dominant factors is their "relationship" with their teacher, such as how comfortable they feel, how much they feel respected, and how much they feel as though the teacher is truly vested in their success.[135] All those are ineffable human matters of *artistry*. We can instruct educators on the research that they need to make their students feel respected, and we can even suggest techniques for doing so, but it ultimately will come down to one human's ability to interact with a mosaic of students, personalities, psychologies, levels of emotional development, etc.

If I am to write another book on education, it might well attempt to capture in greater depth the artistry of teaching rather than the science. But for now, as I move into a discussion of the science about what makes for effective teaching, I simply want to emphasize that there's an ephemeral, ineffable, and artistic element to being a good teacher to which I will not be speaking. Why? Because there are already many gifted educators out there who are great artists but who need the science to channel their artistic skills in the most powerful directions.

QUALIFICATION TWO: THIS ISN'T A HOW-TO

My goal moving forward is to show *what* education should look like and *why* it needs to look that way. While I also want to impress upon you that such a vision is possible, and even relatively easy to implement, this isn't a how-to book for educators. Dave and I work hard when consulting with educators to help them understand all of the detailed ins and outs of the pedagogies that follow, and a how-to book might be forthcoming, but for this text I just want to show you what the pedagogies are, why they make sense, and that implementing them is entirely plausible.

For that matter, I also need to note that dissecting a holistic vision of teaching into its "different" elements is like unscrambling an egg. Even though many of the pedagogies that follow can exist independently of one another, I'm ultimately showing how they all integrate into one greater vision. It's not necessarily the only vision of a better educational structure, but it's mine. I want you to get the gist of the greater vision, and if an isolated idea here or there leaves questions behind, remember again that this isn't a how-to.

CHOKE HOLDS

The United States has been criticized for producing a generation of inflexible thinkers, students who can memorize and regurgitate, but who are incapable of manipulating information in order to answer questions in novel and innovative ways. This is due in part to the fact that our educational system relies on high-stakes standardized testing as a measure of its efficacy, and because today's parents simply are not allowing their child to muck about in the unpleasant, messy, experience of failure long enough to come to terms with the shortcomings of A and formulate plans B, C, D, and E. Lots of kids can ace a test using plan A, but it's going to be the kid who has tried and failed and regrouped in order to try again with twenty-five other plans who will create true innovation and change in our world. That kid is not only creative and innovative in his thinking; he is also unafraid to try out new strategies. He will have the courage and resolve to work through thousands of miscalculations as he pursues a working solution. He will be able to regroup in the face of repeated failures and like Thomas Edison, he will learn the lessons inherent in discovering the thousands of ways a lightbulb does NOT work before inventing the one lightbulb that does.
–Jessica Lahey, *The Gift of Failure*

"Everybody has a plan until they get punched in the face."
–Mike Tyson

Aside from teaching academically, I also teach martial arts, and my students frequently suffer my martial arts analogies. I'm afraid I must subject you to them now, as well. You see, teaching people to contend with being choked reveals a great deal about how to teach *everything to everyone*. For most newcomers, the first time they feel someone's hands around their throat is a revealing moment, even when done gently (as it should be at first). It provokes powerful emotional and psychological responses, which are entirely natural because it makes people feel extraordinarily vulnerable. Some people just shut down, others have cried or needed to step away, and others become remarkably aggressive—all manifestations of the F3 response of fight, flight, or freeze.

What's even more interesting is that some "highly experienced" martial artists, sometimes black belts of multiple degrees, react the same way if, despite years of training, no one ever *really* choked them. Even *they* can freeze or flee, often completely forgetting techniques they trained many times over.

And that's *exactly* what happens to nearly all of my first-year writing students when they get their first papers back with grades of Fs and, for the rare students, Ds. They freak out. I've had students cry, stomp out of the room once class ended, and some have certainly dropped my class that very same day. At first glance, those reactions might seem reasonable. Fs might seem harsh, after all—an unnecessarily draconian measure.

But there's no *real* chokehold here; it's actually a gentle simulation. You see, as I explained to them on the first day of class, as it says in my syllabus, and as I reminded them a number of other times before they submitted the first paper, only the best grade they earn for that essay will count, and that will typically come after multiple rewrites, and typically on the last day of class. Nevertheless, seeing the F or the D, they feel failure's academically lethal grip around their throats, often for the first time.

In fact, the more emotional reactions I've witnessed actually happen at the more prestigious schools, or more among Honors students than non-honors students. Those students are more like the black belts who had never really been choked in their training; they are unaccustomed to hard academic attacks, and they are surprised that all of the techniques they practiced for years have suddenly failed them.

I want to make it clear that I'm not out to provoke negative reactions, per se; the reaction isn't the goal. But I don't mind it either. There are a number of reasons for that, and the rest of this book will explain them directly or indirectly. The first, however, is that the most important lesson students *need*, the one that supersedes all others, is how to fail, learn from that failure, and try again. Students who cannot do that can never go on to do *anything* meaningful. It's the first and most essential lesson.

There have been a lot of terms used of late for that ability to fail and keep going—self-discipline, personal responsibility, determination, etc.—with Angela Duckworth's term, *grit*, having garnered the most attention. But I'm going to use the term *resilience* as a generic umbrella for all of the above.

If resilience's importance seems in any way secondary compared with academic skill sets or academic knowledge, then consider that the National Association of Colleges and Employers' 2017 survey found that of the top seventeen factors that employers considered important in a would-be hire, only *two* pertained to knowledge: "technical skills" and "computer skills," and they both sat low on the list. In contrast, by this point you know what ranked highest: "problem solving." But many of the other traits on the list pertained to *resilience*, such as "work ethic," "initiative," and "adaptability." In other words, and to refer back to Tyson, traits that speak to what their employees would do when they got punched in the face.

Life is full of frustrations and triumphs, with tears and laughter, with moments that empower us and ones that shake us. That's true with friends and relationships, with jobs, with losing our parents and seeing our children born…and it should be no less true with education. I've never worked at a university where I haven't seen students crying to a faculty member, or at least sharing deep emotional strain, about something *non*-academic: a breakup, a lost loved one, financial aid, a roommate…you name it. No one in academia will be surprised by that. Those personal tribulations are expected.

But shouldn't *education itself* penetrate student psyches as deeply?

If education is to prepare students for *life*, if it is to make them live life *better*, then mustn't it equally confront them with the same range of emotions, challenges, failures, and successes that *life* will? This second half of the book will speak to how to do so, for if education fails to prepare students for life, then it fails at its most important goal entirely. Teaching students resilience is not only the most important thing they need, it is also the most compassionate thing we can do—they need to be able to respond effectively when the choke holds come.

As I said, I'm hardly the first to bring attention to the need for resilience development in education. The buzzing conversation, to use Angela Duckworth's language, concerns "perseverance and passion for long-term goals...working strenuously toward challenges, maintaining both effort and interest over years and years—despite failure, adversity, and even just stalls in progress. The gritty individual approaches achievement as a marathon; his advantage is stamina. Whereas disappointment or boredom signals to others that it is time to change trajectory and cut losses, the gritty individual stays the course."[136] Duckworth's *grit* has garnered considerable attention, in part through the work of Carol Dweck. Dweck studied cadets at West Point and found that the biggest predictor of whether or not they would stay versus drop out was not scholastic aptitude or intelligence, but *grit*.

However, there's a lot of question as to whether or not the term *grit* itself is really the one we want. When more precisely studied relative to other factors, "grit as a predictor of performance and success and as a focus of interventions holds much intuitive appeal, but grit as it is currently measured does not appear to be particularly predictive of success and performance."[137] Other researchers arrive at the same conclusion, finding weak if nonexistent relationships between *grit* and academic success.[138] It's not that the general traits within-that-thing-we-call-grit are not useful—they are and we need pedagogies that foster them. Rather, the problem is that "grit," as a single term, might suffer from the *jangle fallacy*,[139] meaning that it comprises far too many different traits within itself.

So, let me throw some other terminology at you:

- Even back in 1995, researchers found that out of thirty-two character traits, only "self-discipline" predicted academic success in college better than students' SAT scores.[140]
- Other research finds that of the "Big Five" personality traits—Openness, Conscientiousness, Extraversion, Agreeableness, and Neuroticism—three predict academic performance—Conscientiousness and Agreeableness positively, and Neuroticism negatively.[141] Of those, "conscientiousness is the most robust predictor."[142]
- Another meta-analytic study found *academic self-efficacy* to be the strongest character trait related to academic success.[143]
- Yet another study identified multiple terms that had been in practice for years, including "self-control", "cognitive self-regulation", "effort regulation", "behavioral engagement", "behavioral disaffection", and found that "other self-regulation and engagement variables were stronger predictors of students' grade than was grit."[144]
- As Peter Arthur and Marianne Fallon discussed on our podcasts, "growth mindset" is another important factor in whether or not students succeed. Students who believe that their ability to learn math is fixed—you either "get math" or you don't—don't do as well as students who believe that it is a flexible skill, that they just aren't good at math "yet." (The ability to add "yet" to a skill is a simple yet great signifier of a growth mindset rather than a fixed one.)

In addition to encompassing all of the above, another reason that *grit* might fail to predict higher academic achievement is that it subsumes what is also just hard work. High-performing students may possess exceptional work ethics, *but studying hard isn't the same thing as being gritty.* In current academic constructs, high-performing students might not fail much, which means they might possess a great work ethic in that they study hard, but little grit in that they always receive good grades (see again: grade inflation).

In contrast to working hard, what we're really seeking is the trait of "being able to get up even when you've failed; it's knowing when to admit defeat and always being ready to try something new."[145] It's what you do *after* you've been punched in the face. Whether "grit" specifically or not, therefore, the greater point is that *resilience*— metacognition, grit, self-discipline, growth mindset, etc.—matters.

Dave and I learned a hard lesson about just how much *resilience* matters. When we were working at a university, we developed and ran a maniacally challenging program that was effectively a critical thinking learning community. Initially, we recruited students by looking at their GPAs, even though, in actuality, our program never got the highest-performing students coming out of high school. Those students went to the university's Honors program. Nevertheless, we selected students with some of the higher remaining GPAs, which put them at better than average. We'd call the students, explain the program to them, and ask them to join.

That approach failed miserably. The students didn't like the program, and many didn't do very well. Why not? Because they knew we selected them based on their strong GPAs, which made them feel special. We unintentionally told them how great they were, so they didn't expect to face hard challenges. They expected that their existing skills, the ones that produced those strong GPAs in high school, would bring them relatively easy success. They couldn't have been more wrong.

So, we changed our recruiting tactics. Instead of inviting students to join the program, we contacted students and told them they were allowed, if they wished, to *apply*. In order to apply, they needed to write an essay discussing a challenge or hardship they had to overcome. And let me tell you, in addition to things like losing a grandparent and that really hard science class, we heard about some serious hardships: rape, disease, homelessness, etc. Some of the essays were heartbreaking and gripping.

But we didn't choose students based on the nature of their hardship, nor on the quality of their writing. In fact, there was no real "application process" other than submitting the essay, and every student who submitted that essay (usually about half of those offered the opportunity to do so) was admitted. We didn't care what they wrote about. We cared only that they had the gumption to apply.

With those students, students who nevertheless held the same level of academic credential as the previous cohorts, the program *thrived*. It thrived because their mindset was entirely different. They no longer felt anointed; they felt like they *earned* it. They felt like they were selected because of what they overcame in life. And they came ready to work through challenges. And when they got frustrated or demoralized by initially low grades and high workloads, we'd simply ask them to recall what they wrote about to get into the program. And then we'd remind them that if they could persevere through that, then they certainly could handle our little critical thinking program.

The essential point here is that we didn't really choose students based on their high school performance or writing ability or thinking skills. We really just put them in a mindset of resilience, and that made all the difference.

As this section moves forward, you'll see that all of the pedagogies for which I advocate advance the idea of building resilience as much as critical thinking. It's not the first text to advocate for that, and it also doesn't radically differ from some other emerging models for doing so. Thomas Hoerr,[146] for example, suggests building classes around the following model:

- Establish the environment;
- Set the expectations;
- Teach the vocabulary;
- Create the frustration;
- Closely monitor;
- Reflect and learn.

Duckworth offers a slightly different conception:

- Create a great and abiding interest
- Create an appetite for practice, constantly challenging oneself
- Create a sense of purpose in what you do
- Maintain hope; a confidence in your ability to keep going

It's easy, I think, to see how each of the frameworks above would help foster resilience. Teaching students by "setting expectations… creating frustration…[and asking them to] reflect and learn" certainly would help build humans with the resilience necessary to keep going after a punch in the face, as would fostering a system where students learn to "constantly challenge" themselves. In the abstract, those frameworks seem like exactly what we need.

But what are they in practice? How can we educate around those structures, and is there evidence that it would accomplish the ends we want?

Let's find out.

IT'S NOT *MY* PROBLEM

In order to survive we had to *want* to learn.
–James E. Zull, *The Art of Changing the Brain*

If we are not just going to develop but also build on students' resilience, if we are to create educational structures that "set expectations", "create frustration", and instigate students to "reflect and learn," then we need to stop predicating education on what is known and start predicating it on what *isn't* known: messy, convoluted, complex, ill-defined, long-term, relevant problems. *Wicked* problems that make students think.

Outside of education, there's a rich four-letter word for learning that happens by confronting messy, frustrating problems that demand our reflection and growth: that word is *life*. Life does a great job of confronting all of us, young people included, with tough, challenging, complex, unclear, frustrating, gritty problems about growing up, parents, "adulting," friendships, romance, sex, health, finances, time management…and everything else.

Consider, and this is critical, that in *life*, the problem or question always *precedes* the information to act. Necessity creates invention. Hunger makes us learn to breast feed, then eat solid food, then cook food. Loneliness makes us seek out sandbox playmates, then real friendships, then real romantic relationships. Disease makes us seek out medication and cures. You get the idea. But the central point—the critical point—is that in life, questions and problems always precede information. The only place that doesn't happen is in school.

School is the only place where humans are
asked to learn like they do in school.

Because that's true—because school is distinct from life—inside the Ivory Tower we unfortunately need a special term for the pedagogy that harnesses the way humans evolved to think and learn by being confronted with problems, and that term is *Problem-Based Learning* (PBL)—"an instructional (and curricular) learner-centered approach that empowers learners to conduct research, integrate theory and practice, and apply knowledge and skills to develop a viable solution to a defined problem."[147] In other words, confront students with a problem and let them think their way through it, i.e., life.

Unfortunately, the vast majority of educators don't work with PBL at all, and some who try to do so actually don't. Some educators will say, for example, that they engaged in PBL because they posed questions to their students. But educators ask up to 400 questions a day, and 80 percent of that questioning seeks regurgitation, not *thinking*.[148] Asking questions that require regurgitation differs entirely from challenging students with truly wicked problems. In fact, just asking questions in class, even if they prompt critical thinking, still isn't actual PBL.

PBL doesn't just ask students a bunch of questions; it *invites students to take part in forming questions*, big questions, questions with no clear answers. As in life, students need to play a role in figuring out what the problems are in the first place, and they need to find the problems that matter to *them*. Once we invite students to help figure out the essential questions, we also instigate them to *think critically* because "central to the process" of getting students thinking "is the students' own formulation of a research question, which they can investigate [and in] this process...negotiate what problems to deal with, enter into continuing dialogues and investigations with each other, and together develop"[149] a solution of some kind.

More simply, problems make brains think. As I discussed in the previous section, confusion or "cognitive disequilibrium" *forces* brains to need to make sense of things. Brains cannot tolerate things not making sense. So, to get students to think, we don't give them information, and we don't even tell them the problem. We first make them figure out what the problem is to begin with, and once *they* discover a problem that matters to *them*, they then *need* to think about it.

So as not to waft about PBL in the abstract any further, here's a very loose notion of how it plays out. Take this example with a grain of salt because, again, my goal here isn't to teach the intricacies of PBL. There are whole books for that. My goal is to impress upon you the need for it and to show you it isn't that hard to achieve. It looks something like this:

"Welcome to Classical Western Philosophy 101. I see you all brought your anthologies to class. Excellent. This semester, you'll work in groups to apply philosophy to a modern issue of your choosing. Your grade will come from a big paper and a long presentation in which you demonstrate your critical thinking about how the philosophers you reference help us solve the modern problem you choose. I'm here if you need help. Have at it."

Note how that invites students to become active agents in their learning by choosing the modern issue they find important and even selecting the philosophers they want to study in solving that problem. As to the educator's role, it's that of a guide. For example, students might not even know what kind of problem to tackle. So, we give them an example of how to start thinking about that. We might explain that philosophy isn't a factor in whether or not the planet is warming, but it *is* a factor in how we are viewing, or should view, the warming of the planet. Furthermore, students might not know how, at first, to even connect a philosopher to a modern problem, so perhaps we give them a short demonstration on how to do so regarding a problem we choose, but never with the problem they chose. The key point is that the students find the problems and the students do the intellectual work of using the source material to solve the problem.

Problem first. Information second.*

In contrast, the dominant paradigm of education, where information precedes the question, is perhaps the most fundamentally flawed and patently ridiculous aspect of all of academia. How can we expect students to think critically if their brains don't encounter the cognitive disequilibrium of a wicked problem? Remember the junkyard. The junk only took on meaning when a problem emerged—a pending attack or snowstorm or tag sale.

Information only ceases to be junk when in a meaningful context, something James Gee masterfully demonstrates in his book, *Situated Learning*. Gee describes how even young children can easily learn the very complex game of Pokémon—a card game with battling monsters, each with different powers, and each with abilities to evolve into other monsters. Totaling the powers and abilities in all the different cards (from Pokémon years ago, when it was even less complex than today), Gee calculated that Pokémon was a system of "150 x 16 x 2 x 8" variables. Yet even young children "could readily name all 150 Pokémon and state their type, skills, and what other Pokémon they could evolve into…. We had no trouble finding children who knew their Pokémon—children as young as five and six."

Now contrast the complexity of Pokémon against the relative simplicity of much of what we try to teach children through didactic instruction, such as facts about America's history or multiplication. The times tables up to ten, for instance, contains only 100 variables even if we count the redundancies (4x6 is the same as 6x4). Yet look at how difficult it is for some children to memorize that. Why? Because it holds neither meaning nor value (that *they* see as immediately relevant to their lives). Pardon my French here, but the kids don't give a shit about times tables. And there's really no reason they should, not as they see it. (I'm not arguing against math, which is *very* important, and I would argue that things like times tables

---

* Truthfully, the question and information start to interact and evolve. The more they learn about the issue, they more they refine, redefine, or entirely change the question, which is how it should be because that's what intellectuals do.

IT'S NOT *MY* PROBLEM

are among the things students *do* need to memorize. But note the difference in getting them to learn times tables versus how readily they will teach themselves the more complex universe of Pokémon.) The point is that kids acquire deep knowledge of Pokémon because they get the information in the context of a problem—they want to win at Pokémon!

How they learn to play Pokémon is also one of the key factors in PBL. Do they get direct instruction on every rule of the game *before* they play? Do they receive a lecture on Pokémon, study all the cards, and need to pass a test? No. *They just start playing* and they learn as they go. That's how we learn everything (outside of school). We start engaging the problem and we learn as we go. We determine a need and then think critically through *expectations, frustrations,* and a need to *reflect* and grow.

Unlike in school, knowledge doesn't come as information-junk before or absent of application. Instead, knowledge comes during the process of solving problems—exactly when we need it. As Michelle Chouinard describes it, children naturally learn best when "children's questions get answers exactly when the children can use them most, when they are open to the information, and when they are trying to resolve a state of disequilibrium. Also, information that the child is ready for or interested in may make the biggest impression in terms of memory and cognitive organization."[150] Thus, and it shouldn't surprise anyone, when information comes when it is wanted, children learn more easily, and can learn a great deal.

In school, on the other hand, educators believe that students need information first in order to solve problems second, if they ever solve problems at all. But that's backwards. Problems and context drive the acquisition of information, giving it purpose. That's what PBL does. It exploits young *homo sapiens* natural need to think when seeing a problem. Like Pokémon, PBL puts students in a context where they naturally acquire information in layers. Returning to our philosophy class, the students start by selecting an initial modern issue as their problem, and they start researching it, and reading the philosophers. But as they understand each one better, the problem deepens and evolves. They might realize that they don't want to reference a philosopher they initially wanted to reference, or add a philosopher, or refocus how they are viewing the modern problem. They start into the problem, get some information, see where there are gaps, gain a stronger understanding of the context, realize what's *needed*, and only then go back for more information. Repeat. Repeat. Repeat *ad infinitum*.

To offer another example of how the problem needs to precede the information, here's one of my own experiences: For years, like many writing teachers, I started my semester by teaching students how to write a thesis statement—a statement about the paper's main idea. I assigned readings about thesis statements and offered what I thought were some pretty darn-tooting awesome presentations and exercises about writing theses. But, invariably, when the students finally submitted their first papers, their theses *sucked*. At best, they were literal replications of what we practiced but lacked needed depth and insight. At worst, the students just didn't write a thesis at all. (I should note that I no longer really work with thesis-driven writing in the classic sense, but that's a different matter.)

The problem was that no matter how well I taught the writing of a thesis, the students lacked an understanding of the problem; because they hadn't written a paper yet, they couldn't see how unfocused their papers would be without a thesis. My thesis lessons amounted to nothing more than presentations on the junkyard's collection of fire hydrants.

So, I turned my approach on its head. I put the problem first. Instead of teaching them how to write a thesis statement, we jumped right into writing papers with virtually no instruction on how to do so. Then, we sat together and examined their papers as a class, grading them together (with an authentic critical thinking standard as the means of assessment, which is essential, and which I'll discuss soon). And two things happened: First, all the papers earned poor grades (most failed). Second, the *students* realized that the poor grades were a result of the fact that the papers lacked focus. *They* couldn't follow one another's papers.

They came to understand the *problem*.

Can you guess what happened next? Every semester, around three weeks into the process and suddenly aloft in the cognitive disequilibrium of not knowing how to focus a paper, the students *asked me* if I could teach them how to develop a thesis. And on a moment's notice, it just so happens that I had exercises ready to go for how to build a thesis statement. (It's almost like I knew they would ask!) And when I taught students how to develop a thesis *after* the students asked me to do so, *after* the students recognized the *problem*, the students were attentive, and interested, and the theses developed fast. It was just Pokémon all over again. Problem first. Information when immediately needed and applicable.

The students usually asked me something else as well. *After* I gave them a lesson on how to develop a thesis, they'd ask me why I didn't just teach them that earlier—*before* they failed their papers. In return, I'd ask them if that lesson would have had as much impact. I asked if they would have appreciated it the same way, or listened as carefully. Invariably, they all said they wouldn't have. *They* understood why they needed to understand the problem before receiving the information.*

Thus, PBL instigates critical thinking and learning by empowering student *agency*. It establishes a problem, provides resources (including texts and teacher), makes the assessment clear (which should be based in critical thinking), and then lets the students have at it.

Hence the title of this chapter. When I say, "It's not my problem," I mean a few different things. On the surface, I mean that when teaching through PBL, I am not going to be the one to determine the problem we tackle. The course might broadly be about a topic, such as Shakespeare or ecology, but the students will need to further

---

* If you're noting here that, in this instance, I offered something akin to a lecture, you'd be right. But, as I noted in my critique of lecture, it has a place, but only in rare instances, only as the exception rather than the rule. This is one such exception.

clarify it, whittle it, modify it, and ultimately wrestle it to the ground. *Their* ownership makes their brains happy. When curiosity runs high, the brain releases more dopamine,[151] which, again, is the feel-good drug, and that makes students *want* to take on challenges, figure out new problems, think critically, and work *harder*.

But when I say, "It's not my problem," I also mean something *much* more important: I mean that it's not up to me to make sure the students learn, i.e., to "teach" them in the classical sense. In PBL, if students don't want to do the reading, or don't want to turn in work, or don't want to X, well then that's really "not my problem."

If you recall the problem educators face with student resistance, such as in trying to get students to do assigned readings, then know that PBL crucially flips that school game on its head. The educator no longer has to enforce the school game because PBL changes school to roughly three moving parts:

1. The problem
2. The resources (texts, teachers, other students, etc.)
3. The grading standard (hopefully based on critical thinking)

It's up to the *students* to use 1 and 2 in order to achieve 3, which means that PBL takes the responsibility away from the teacher to "teach" and puts the onus on the students to learn.

Students: "What happens if we don't do the reading?"

Me: "Not my problem. *I* don't need to solve this problem, you do."

Students: "Well, how much reading do we have to do?"

Me: "Enough to solve the problem."

Students: "When is the reading due?"

Me: "Well, I don't know. You need to start figuring out the problem and you need the reading to do it. So, what do you think?"

Students: "That we need to start doing it right away?"

Me: "Indeed."

That's all an oversimplification and I'm actually extremely supportive, but the greater point remains the same: It's not *my* problem to figure out what the problem should be; it's theirs. And it sure as hell isn't *my* problem to figure out the solutions; it's theirs. If they want to do well, if they want to engage the problem, they'll need to engage the resources. And when they become emotionally and intellectually invested in the problem, then learning becomes *meaningful* instead of contrived. Students learn that it is their critical thinking about the problem, not what they can regurgitate, that's most valued intellectually and academically; I'm just there to help.

And don't you suppose this process of redefining the problem, re-engaging sources, re-conceiving solutions to wicked problems that actually have no one solution builds resilience?

THE EVIDENCE FOR PBL

But don't take my word for it. Ample research demonstrates that PBL improves the long-term retention of knowledge,[152] skill proficiency,[153] student motivation—they actually do much more work with higher intrinsic motivation—and meaning making.[154] In a larger analysis done in medical school, PBL students graduate with "similar factual knowledge but better clinical performance," appreciate increased interaction with other students and faculty, "show a greater tendency to use evidence-based medicine," show gains in "social and cognitive domains," and "work more efficiently."[155] With all of the calls for teaching "soft skills" such as working in teams and communication, PBL should drive every educational institution in the U.S.

In terms of the critical thinking crisis, it probably won't surprise you by now to learn that, whereas the traditional learning in Section I suppresses thinking, PBL shows increased cognitive engagement by students,[156] improved reasoning skills,[157] and, because it typically involves group work, a tremendous amount of development across social indexes.[158] Again, unlike the Rock Master Scott teaching methods that thwart critical thinking, PBL *improves* "cognitive engagement" and "reasoning."

Yet, it's not just the students who benefit; educators get more out of it as well. They report that using PBL improves their own understanding of content. They appreciate the role of facilitator rather than transmitter. And they see "teaching as scholarship".[159] There's really too much research on this to discuss, but the nutshell is that PBL, not surprisingly, taps the way *homo sapiens* evolved to survive though problem solving.

One of the only areas where PBL's results aren't necessarily better than more traditional methods is in short-term memorization and regurgitation.[160] If students need to cram for a multiple-choice test, PBL isn't the way to go. But since those tests are silly, we really shouldn't care.

Still, if all the research I've presented thus far isn't persuasive, then consider the fMRI studies that "have linked the changes of cortical activation pattern to the training of cognitive skills,"[161] which is a highfalutin way of saying that teaching methods alter brain structure. For example, one study[162] looked at the difference between *hypothesis-understanding* students—those who were *told* the hypothesis by the instructor—and *hypothesis-generating* students—those who were taught how to develop their *own* hypotheses. Which group do you suppose developed a better brain, the students told a hypothesis or the students left to devise one? The group that had to develop their own hypothesis, i.e., think for themselves, showed *positive changes in their brains after just two months of training.* But the other group, the group that was told the idea instead of generating it, didn't.

And before I move off that point, there's ample research now about our amazingly neuroplastic brains, which continuously rewrite themselves based on everything we do in our lives. If we do a lot of short-term memorization, our brains develop pathways for that. If we need to memorize useless facts, our brains develop pathways for that. If we need to suppress boredom while sitting in chairs and staring at screens, our brains develop pathways for that. Consider, therefore, not only the catastrophic opportunity loss in terms of the students' brains we could be developing, consider the cognitive castration of taking brains designed for critical thinking and cutting them down to information-memorizers.

I hope this clarifies and emphasizes that for students, the Section I construct, the Rock-Master-Scott construct, is *madness*. In school—and *only* in school—are young humans affronted by massive quantities of information to remember, or books to read, or equations to learn, not just before a meaningful problem emerges, but typically, and worse, where no problem ever emerges that would induce their brains to do what brains enjoy doing, what brains evolved to do best: think. Reason contextually. Learn meaningfully and purposefully. That is why, as Jackson Nickerson of the *Brookings Institute* said during one of *The Critical Thinking Initiative* podcast episodes, Rock Master Scott practices aren't neutral. "We are not doing no harm. We are *doing harm* to students if we are training them" to regurgitate "right" answers instead of building their brains to discover and think critically through wicked problems.

But as I've shown, we can use PBL to cultivate rich brains, brains built on complex, messy, wicked, thoughtful, timely, meaningful problems.

SCHLEPPING WOOD

Consider starting work on a construction site. You possess *no* construction experience, so your first jobs aren't the sexiest: Perhaps, all you are asked to do at first is schlepp wood—new lumber to where they need it, scrap lumber to the dumpster. Now that's hardly exciting work. It's not even skilled labor. But there is something very important about that work: it *matters.* No matter how basic, it nevertheless makes you part of a community, and though it's arguably the easiest, most unglorified work, it's work that still contributes to the group's success.

In academia's traditional constructs, on the other hand, perhaps the most dominant of all lessons, perhaps the taproot of *indifference* itself, is that *students know that what they think doesn't matter to the greater community.* Students predominantly, almost exclusively, learn about ideas other people already devised. They know that they will not affect the field, much less even the direction of the class or the thinking of the professor. Unlike the day-one construction worker who, though only carrying wood, knows that they meaningfully contribute to their group's greater success, our students know that what they learn and what they think will affect *nothing.* At best, in a group discussion, a student might affect a peer's thinking about the Vietnam War, but that won't change how anyone dates because that's not what Section 1 education is for anyway—it's not about life.

Many educators recognize this intuitively, if not explicitly. To compensate for their students' utter irrelevance, many educators offer praise for work, such as "this is really interesting!" or "You've really got me thinking here!" But when has a student *ever* seen a professor *meaningfully* change a lesson, much less a class or course, or worldview, because of how that student supposedly "got them thinking"? Never.

Unfortunately, "attempting to boost students' self-esteem with words is less effective than asking them to persevere on a challenging task"[163] in which students feel they can accomplish something *meaningful*. Students easily see through well-intentioned placations. What they want is what is *meaningful* to the construction worker (and to all of us): authentic intellectual and social relevancy. What students want, in contrast, as one educator put it, is "not a professor-student relationship but a senior colleague-junior colleague...relationship... [where teachers and students are] investigating this subject together... sharing the learning process."[164]

Now some educators will contend that they *do*, in fact, create social learning environments: group projects, class discussions, student feedback, etc. But those don't necessarily involve real social relevancy because people "whose contributions are never adopted" or are not "active participants in the practices of a social community" eventually realize that they really don't matter. Bourgeoning members of any community "whose contributions are never adopted develop an identity of non-participation that progressively marginalizes them. Their experience becomes irrelevant because it cannot be asserted and recognized as a form of competency."[165] Thus, students know they remain "marginalized" and "irrelevant" because they are not "active participants in the practices of a social community." Their ideas are "*never* adopted." They are learning about history but not "bourgeoning" historians who use history to affect their lives, our world, or even our understanding of history itself.

That's yet another reason why a construct such as PBL (or others like it) works. It makes students *matter*. It makes their critical thinking acquire intellectual relevance and *power*. *They* define the problem. And since there is no one right answer to the problem, the *students* invariably bring forward solutions the educators never even considered. *Students* can even affect the course schedule in ways that suit their needs to deepen their approach to the problem. It's pretty clear from volumes of research that the best learning is an "encompassing process of being active participants in the practices of social communities and constructing identities in relation to these communities,"[166] which is exactly what PBL allows.

None of this means that students need to feel like equals; they *know* they are not our equals. But they don't need to be. They just need to *matter*—to schlepp wood.

For example, one of the ways I make students matter is to grade papers *with* them, not only inviting them to see what *I* do, but ultimately having them join me in the process itself as stakeholders and contributors. So, from the first paper forward, we sit together as a class and collectively grade one another's papers.*

At first, grading together sure isn't democratic. New students don't know a lick about what makes a decent essay, and they don't yet understand my critical thinking standards. (If you're asking why I don't teach those standards first and then have them write the paper, please refer back to the previous chapter. Problem first. Information second.) With rare exception, students *know* they are not my equal. So, we don't operate under any pretenses that they know as much as I do. But they don't need my level of expertise for us to start a conversation. In contrast, the fact that they lack expertise is exactly *why* we all need to converse.

After just a short while, students can grade papers fairly accurately and offer meaningful advice to one another in order to help each other succeed. They begin to acquire authentic social and intellectual relevancy to the group, the course, and the field. Students also quickly become so adept at reading essays that they affect *my* thinking about the grades. Talk about relevancy! Imagine how powerful it is for my students when I say, earnestly, "Hey. That's a great point. I hadn't seen that. You're making me rethink this." And then their comment actually affects the grade; it might even determine the grade. Once students can start doing that, usually around mid-semester, I can walk into a grading workshop, sit down, listen, and leave without saying a word. The students can grade one another's papers by

---

* We don't grade all of the students' papers together every time they submit. That would just consume too much time. But every student gets at least one paper graded by the class.

themselves. They can help one another too. They attained real social and intellectual relevancy. They *matter* to one another because they help one another and even grade one another.

So, I work with *apprentices,* not students. I work with capable intellectuals who, at first, possess neither the knowledge nor skills to contribute much, but who can soon become meaningful, important, active members of a community where their ideas *matter,* where *they* matter, as *people.*

Given that students otherwise know they do not matter, is it hard to see how anti-intellectualism emerged in our country? Academia made it very clear to generations of people that they really aren't welcome in intellectual discourse. They can learn the things other people thought —things that will not help them on their next date— but they cannot contribute to the intellectual world. They cannot affect that academic world. They can't even truly alter the thinking of their educators. They can't even schlepp the lumber.

Thus, academia resigned nearly all of its learners, Ph.D. students excepted, to being the *other,* to studying the intellectual world instead of joining it. We've made them learn about philosophers instead of teaching them to philosophize. We've made them learn about history instead of making each and every one of them historians who actionalize history in their own lives. Even in the sciences, where I previously described how much learning is still through *rote* or canned experiments, we taught them to understand science rather than innovate it. We didn't learn this simple lesson put elegantly by Amanda Ripley:

Humans need to be heard before they will listen.

F'EM

Ever tried.
Ever failed.
No matter.
Try again.
Fail again.
Fail better.
—Samuel Beckett

As I alluded to earlier with respect to *resilience*, one of the more critical flaws in traditional perfunctory learning is how it treats failure: Failure is typically high stakes because there's typically just one chance at the big exam, which makes it terminal. That's why failing in school can make students feel like "failures".

Because education sets failure up as something so negative, traditional learning is predicated on preventing failure, and one of the ways that occurs is by permitting students to pass assignments with only 60 percent proficiency (or something thereabouts), the rough equivalent of a D. With 60 percent proficiency being "passing," students don't "fail," so they can progress to the next learning experience, but having not-failed doesn't mean they mastered the material.

Sal Khan offers my favorite analogy for this kind of education:

> *To appreciate how absurd that is, imagine if we did other things in our life that way. Say, home-building. So, we bring in the contractor and say, "We were told we have two weeks to build a foundation. Do what you can." So, they do what they can. Maybe it rains. Maybe*

some of the supplies don't show up. And two weeks later, the inspector comes, looks around, says, "OK, the concrete is still wet right over there, that part's not quite up to code...I'll give it an 80 percent." You say, "Great! That's a C. Let's build the first floor." Same thing. We have two weeks, do what you can, inspector shows up, it's a 75 percent. Great, that's a D-plus. Second floor, third floor, and all of a sudden, while you're building the third floor, the whole structure collapses. And if your reaction is the reaction you typically have in education, or that a lot of folks have, you might say, maybe we had a bad contractor, or maybe we needed better inspection or more frequent inspection. But what was really broken was the process. We were artificially constraining how long we had to learn something, pretty much ensuring a variable outcome....

Only academia would develop such an unnatural, dysfunctional concept of learning that predetermines the amount of time a heterogony of students will spend learning something, and that advances them to the next subject before *mastering* the first one. Such a system, if not designed to create inequity (which it was), certainly guarantees that inequity will dominate. It quickly separates the Eloi from the Morlocks, and it makes it harder and harder every year for those behind to catch up.

It also sends the message that it's fine to go through life without really mastering things. Learning 75 percent is good enough. Hardly the lesson we want to send to our would-be-anythings—carpenters, plumbers, nurses, parents, mechanics, etc.

Finally, it presumes that those who learn fastest learn best. And sometimes that's true. Other times, people might learn more slowly but when something clicks, they end up with the most skill. Consider, for example, that Michael Jordan wasn't the best basketball player on his high school team. He got kicked off. Basketball didn't "click" for him as fast as for some others, but when it did...

COGNITIVE THREAT

Khan's analogy to the "broken process" of perfunctory learning only speaks to part of the problem. Yes, eventually, the house collapses, but for students this time-based, high-stakes model also causes considerable *cognitive stress.*

Stress is not *necessarily* bad. It depends on whether it is embraced as a *challenge* or perceived as a *threat.* Students who experience stress as a *challenge* actually become excited about learning *(homo Sapiens* evolved to embrace challenges) and might even learn more as a result. Alternatively, when stress results in students feeling surprised, feeling out of control, and/or lacking the needed resources, then it attacks them as a *threat.* When students perceive *threat,* it triggers the *F3* response—fight, flight, or freeze—*which shuts down higher cognitive ability.* Students under threat *can't* think critically.

To understand why *threat* inhibits critical thinking, consider a small part of our brains called the *amygdala,* which, in simple terms, is a switch that *either* activates the *prefrontal cortex*—the thinking part of our brains—or activates the lower brain—the part concerned with just keeping us alive: *"Don't stop to think! Run!"* When the *amygdala* feels threatened, it directs activity *away* from the *prefrontal cortex* and toward the lower brain because, at such times, it doesn't want to engage intellectual ideas; it just wants to live.

The amygdala's control over which part of the brain gets to be in control is powerful, powerful because our brains house more neural wiring running *from* the amygdala *to* the *prefrontal cortex* than from the *prefrontal cortex* to the *amygdala,* which means that the *amygdala* tells the *prefrontal cortex* what to do, not the other way about. If you've ever felt so emotional that you "couldn't think straight," or if you ever wondered why your emotions got the better of you when you "knew better," now you know why: the *amygdala,* when perceiving threat, turned off your thinking brain. Choke holds, again.

Returning to academia, and as I noted earlier, stress that the amygdala perceives as *challenge* does not negatively affect performance, and some evidence suggests it might even improve it.[167] Meanwhile, stress perceived from *threat* produces poor performance,[168] even to the degree of *reducing* blood flow to the brain ("Get blood to the legs. We need to run!"), and even activating *pain* receptors.[169] That warrants repeating: When students perceive a situation as threatening, their lower brain becomes more activated, the blood to their brain reduces, and their *pain* receptors activate! School, if threatening, hurts. Simply put, "when a student is given a cognitively challenging problem to attend to…the brain may see the assignment or the task as a threat; then, the fight or flight system is active, [which] can impede cognitive reasoning."[170]

As Paul Tough explains in *How Children Succeed: Grit, Curiosity, and the Hidden Power of Character,*

> A fear of failure can poison learning by creating aversions to the kinds of experimentation and risk taking that characterize striving, or by diminishing performance under pressure, as in a test setting…. Students who have a high fear of making errors when taking tests may actually do worse on the text because of their anxiety. Why? It seems that a significant portion of their working memory capacity is expended to monitor their performance (How am I doing? Am I making mistakes?), leaving less working memory capacity available to solve the problems posed by the test.[171]

Thus, many students find traditional school threatening. And they should. Consider the construct:

- You have one week until the test, with no control over that timing, and you might not have mastered the previous content on which this test depends, so you're already working at a deficit.
- You have one chance to take the test (high stakes!).
- You'll need to learn the information through lecture, which

bores and hurts your brain, and if that lecture presents the information very clearly, it makes it harder for you to learn the information.

- It's on 73 facts about the French and Indian War. You don't give a shit about the French and Indian War. The information has no relevance to any of your other classes, and certainly not to your next date.

- A portion of those 73 facts are the important ones—they will be on the test. But you won't know which of the 73 facts are actually important until you get to the test. It's a Jack-in-the-Box.

- If it is an essay test or paper, you probably face bigger problems: You probably don't really know how you'll be graded. Even if the teacher wants you to "analyze thoroughly," as I demonstrated before, you don't really know what this teacher means by that (and the teacher might not either).

If we set out to design an educational system that our children's brains would find more threatening, we'd be hard pressed to do so.

CONTROL AND MASTERY LEARNING

If we want students' brains to get out of their own way and stop failing tests because they're worried about tests, we need to create challenge-stress, not threat-stress. Challenge-stress requires keeping the *amygdala* happy. But "happy" in amygdala terms is not what *you* might think, nor is it what many *educators* think.

Efforts by educators to create happy students through happy classrooms, including efforts to entertain students through the use of tablets, gamification, or other means, not only prove ineffective, they might prove counterproductive. Many educators try to bring "positive emotions back into the classroom...and stir up students' emotions in artificial and non-task related ways, such as by telling jokes, showing cartoons, doling out prizes...[but] emotions that are

irrelevant to tasks at hand may actually interfere [with learning]."[172]
Why? Because jokes don't change the *fundamental, threat-inducing
construct of most contemporary education.*

Instead of trying to distract the threatened amygdala with jokes,
games, and sparkly electronics (none of which works), we can actually
make the amygdala *genuinely* happy, and happy, for an amygdala,
always means *control.*[173] Oh, how the amygdala loves *control,* which
occurs not through a lack of stress, but when educators do a few very
simple things that neuroscience values in making sure that stress is
a *challenge:*

- "give assignments that require significant time and effort
  from students
- Ensure substantive interaction among students and with the
  instructor
- Involve a cycle of assignments with instructor feedback and
  student response to that feedback
- Involve substantive reflection and integration of learning by
  students
- Require that students apply learning to real-world cases,
  project, simulations, and so on."[174]

You might immediately recognize that last bullet as problem-
based learning, which research tells us students find *challenging* instead
of *threatening.*[175]

But the rest of that list overlaps seamlessly with *mastery learning,*
which is another fancy educational term for the kind of learning we
do in life all the time. *Mastery learning* involves doing one thing until
you "master" it before moving to the next, more challenging level,
i.e., making sure the house's foundation is actually done right before
building the first floor. Mastery learning involves a simple cycle: a
challenge, the time and resources to attempt the challenge, the ability
to reflect, and the opportunity to try again.

As part of that *mastery* process, that *life* process, we also *always* do something else, something that is the most important learning tool of all: we *fail*. Unlike most education, however, *mastery learning* does not confront students with one-time high-stakes assessments, and it does not let students pass with just 60 percent aptitude.

Instead, *mastery learning* provides students with multiple chances to *fail forward*. *Failing forward* means multiple no-stakes or low-stakes opportunities to succeed, control over how time is spent, control over when to make attempts, control over the use of resources, feedback when it is needed, etc. When that happens, "failure" isn't terminal. Failure is opportunity. It's the *challenge* to continue improving until "mastering" what needs mastering. Even if the semester ends and students haven't earned an A or achieved real "mastery," the control they gain over the process, and the opportunity to fail forward, still improves their outcomes and experience.

Why is this so important? Because "motivation can remain *high* if a student explains his poor performance in terms of controllable and temporary causes such as inadequate preparation, insufficient effort, or lack of relevant information. Under these circumstances, students can maintain the belief that they are capable of changing their behaviors to achieve the most positive outcomes."[176] Put another way, with resources, time, and low-to-no-stakes failure opportunities, *threats* become *challenges*.

So that mastery learning doesn't remain completely abstract, here's one high-level, grain-of-salt example of how it could look in academia—which presently doesn't permit unlimited time to master material (because the next semester is coming regardless). In a traditional class based on perfunctory learning, all students complete all of the course elements. Let's say that involves, for the sake of example, four elements: an exam, a short paper, another exam, and a long paper. Student grades would vary from As down to who knows what. And then a final grade would average all of the grades (perhaps some weighted more than others).

In this example of a mastery model, students must earn high score (should read: students must earn a high score) (95+, 90+, or some other high mark) on the first exam, with as many opportunities to retest as needed, before being permitted to move onto the first paper, and then a mastery grade on the first paper before moving onto the second exam. The grade for the course becomes based on how many assignments the student masters, for example, an F for none, a D for one, a C for two, a B for three, and an A for all four.

Now this model does require a restructuring of course elements in more ways than I can describe here, but one key element I will speak to is that it just requires educators to prioritize what needs to be learned, so that the most essential elements, the baselines, come first. In a sense, the course becomes simplified by two questions: What are the minimum things a student must "master" to exit the course (grade C)? And what would you like to see students really "master" to excel (grade A)?

The concern, and sometimes objection, to this model that immediately emerges from many educators is that all students do not learn, or at least are not assessed on, all of the course elements. Those earning a C might only be exposed to, and certainly will only be tested on, information for the first two assessments (exam one and paper one). That's true. But here's the rub—the very important rub: As I noted earlier, under popular traditional methods, students forget half of what they learned within a semester, and within two years, A students remember about as much as C students (which isn't much at all). So the argument that students need to learn everything the course covers is a myth. *They forget it anyway.* It isn't really *learned.* That's why researchers argue that we immediately engage students with "deep learning"—and mastery is one kind of deep learning— and, equally, "sacrifice breadth for depth."[177] As they put it, "It is important to remember that although we hate to 'give up' some of our favorite topics, the topics that are only covered in passing are not meaningfully retained. Thus we have already given them up; it just has not been obvious." In other words, the mastery model doesn't sacrifice any knowledge.

If anything, it does the opposite. To distill it down to a somewhat oversimplified tradeoff, would we rather have students learn less course material deeply or more course material frailly, if at all? And that's for the students who earn a C. For the A students, the mastery model allows them not to learn less, but to learn more, and *more deeply than before.*

Now here's where mastery learning gets even more meaningful: What's one of, if not the biggest, predictors of student success? Engagement.[178] What's the biggest predictor of engagement? A *mastery attitude* in the students (which means intrinsic motivation to develop real skills rather than just get a good grade).[179] And what's one of the biggest predictors about a mastery attitude in students? Teachers. Teachers who

(a) assign 'challenge tasks' [that] encourage students to invest, make an effort, and think;
(b) [encourage] students to ask questions and seek help from different resources...
(c) [are] enthusiastic, and
(d) [give] different assignments to different students.

Teachers who, more generally, treat students as intellectuals, take their ideas seriously, build meaningful relationships with them, and give them control so their amygdalas relax, enabling them to *think*.[180] (Doesn't that harken back to PBL?)

That autonomy is essential for many reasons, not the least of which being that it affords students an opportunity they seldom have in school, the opportunity to enter a *flow state*. Coined by Mihaly Csikszentmihalyi, a flow state is a condition of optimal mental performance, one in which we become so focused on the task at hand that the rest of the world temporarily disappears. If you've ever lost yourself in a task for a period of time but been highly productive nevertheless, that's a flow state, and if you've ever seen a child consumed in a task for a couple hours before coming up for air, e.g., building LEGO, then you've seen a flow state in action.

As for the research on mastery learning,* there's not enough of it but the evidence shows improved outcomes relative to traditional models, especially in terms of closing achievement gaps for low-performing students. And one of the most oft-cited studies, a 1990 meta-analysis of over one hundred other studies, found mastery learning beneficial in 93 percent of the studies in which students were tested against a final exam.[181] But what's far more important is the abundant research showing that mastery learning improves student motivation, self-regulation, metacognition, and other higher-order factors related to learning, which also just so happen to be the qualities we want to see developed in humans anyway.

Whatever you've achieved in your life, is it because of the 73 facts you learned about the French and Indian War, or because you learned to embrace challenges, exercise your time and resources wisely, fail, reflect, and try again until you succeeded? If you could build a human (such as your child) who knew a lot of stuff or a human who embraced the challenge of failing forward, which would you choose?

---

* I want to note that there are different formal models of mastery learning that cycle through specific steps from pre-assessment through final assessment. This is not a commentary on those alone but on the general premise of mastery learning even if it doesn't, and sometimes shouldn't, follow one particular cycle.

IT'S CRITICAL THINKING, STUPID (PART 2)

I want to oppose the idea that the school has to teach directly that special knowledge and those accomplishments which one has to use directly later in life. The demands of life are much too manifold to let such a specialized training in school appear possible [...] The development of general ability for independent thinking and judgement should always be placed foremost.
   —Albert Einstein

Having put it off until now, I think it's high time that I finally speak directly to what teaching critical thinking involves. I'll offer the foundations, but I cannot explain the specific critical thinking ecosystem that Dave and I developed. We have another text for that, one suited for those who want to implement the system. You don't need to be mired down in those details, but you'll probably appreciate the big picture.

Furthermore, the principles I proffer here afford themselves to anyone or any institution that might want to build critical thinking into their infrastructure. I'll reference our system vaguely, but I don't presume that it's the only one, and any organization can exercise the principles here to build something that might be new and better.

If there's some good news when it comes to higher education's critical thinking crisis, it's that academia has at least started to take notice. Dave and I increasingly receive calls from institutions, K-Ph.D., that are launching critical thinking initiatives. Some of these are large-scale efforts. But too many others, as written in the article, *Study: Nearly Half of Millennials Get an 'F' in Critical Thinking*, fall more into "a band-aid approach" in which "colleges and universities [add] a required course or two" to solve the critical thinking problem, and nothing more.[182] Though less than ideal, that single course can still be an important step in the right direction, so let's celebrate it.

However, if campuses really want "to solve the problem, critical thinking pedagogy must flow through all curricula—professional, STEM and liberal arts."[183] Dave and I, in fact, call for education to be a *critical thinking ecosystem*—an environment where every facet works in harmony around the goal of supporting the critical thinker.

To understand why that harmony matters so much, think of a student not as a person, per se, but as a young, little brain that wants to grow into a big brain.* In order to grow and mature, Little Brain doesn't need food, water, and shelter, but rather pedagogy, assignments, and assessments that foster critical thinking. Unfortunately, Little Brain not only finds an environment lacking *one* such element, it finds an environment lacking *every* needed element. As explained in Section I,

- the *pedagogies* by which students are taught are at best "hopeful" because faculty "do not teach critical thinking *per se*," and because of lectures that are "painful," and because other pedagogies actually penalize the student who wants to make sense of the world
- *subject matter* is approached through *confusion* and *indifference*, where no subject relates to any other, and where no subject relates directly to the students' lives
- *assignments* ask for memorization in the form of tests or summary in the form of written assignments
- *assessments*, which typically inflate grades, do not hinge on students' ability to think critically and make meaning, but on "right" answers about memorizing information-junk

---

* This is a similar analogy and set of information we provide in our textbooks and online training modules.

- students entirely lack instruction on a direct *method* for actually approaching the world through a critical thinking process, and are only "immersed" in methods that educators hope will get their "critical thinking juices flowing." But "students who have not been taught a demanding, challenging, thinking curriculum do poorly on tests of reasoning or problem solving."[184]

The failing ecosystem described above, that of Section I, not only fails to help Little Brain grow, it's virtually trying to kill Little Brain. It's *cognitively dystopic.* One might be hard pressed to design an educational ecosystem more hostile than that to Little brain that wants to become a big brain.

But it's not because educators don't *care.* And it's not because they don't *try.* Again, educators nobly work too hard for too little reward and with insufficient support. They also lack the luxury I possess, which is the time to study critical thinking directly. And even if they had the time, they might be as interested in reading peer-reviewed research on teaching methods as I would be in teaching first grade, which is *not at all.* (And our society needs *many* more dedicated first-grade teachers than it does professional pedagogues such as me. Their job is much harder than mine and much more important.) The reality is that most educators *want* their students to think critically, and to be engaged, and find education meaningful, and to attain high standards, etc. They know they don't understand what's involved, but they want to learn and need the tools.[185]

BUILDING A CRITICAL THINKING ECOSYSTEM TO NOURISH LITTLE BRAIN

As other researchers put it, "the effective implementation of critical thinking through curriculum, pedagogy, and assessment requires a complex and holistic approach."[186] We need to embrace the fact that cultivating critical thinking "requires both the willingness to incorporate [critical thinking] instruction and explicit strategies and skills to do it effectively."[187] We need to integrate critical thinking as the common driving force across academia, and to do that demands an ecosystem that is:

- An educational *holon*
- Neurobiological
- Metacognitive
- Interdisciplinary, and
- Generative

AN EDUCATIONAL HOLON

A *holon* is something in which every part of the whole has all of the properties of the whole. In the educational sense, a critical thinking holon would look something like this:

Assignments would not only need to ask for critical thinking, they would need to make critical thinking the far-and-above dominant act that is required.

But more imperative than *assignments* are *assessments*. This is because, more than any other factor, it is *assessments* that determine how students approach their learning.[188] Whereas research shows that most faculty do not use a critical thinking rubric,[189] research also, and not surprisingly, shows that when educators teach students to think critically relative to a rubric, critical thinking actually improves.[190,191,192]

But merely using a thinking *assessment* isn't enough; students still must understand what critical thinking is and be taught a method of doing it. In terms of a thinking *method*, meta-analyses show that when given direct instruction on *methods* of critical thinking, students' abilities to think critically actually improves.[193]

Of course, not one single syllable of any of this should be surprising to anyone. It should only make sense that if we want students to improve as critical thinkers, we should predicate their education on it by assigning it, teaching it, practicing it, and assessing it.

However, just having each of those parts in place doesn't really create a *holon*. If there's a *method* for students to learn how to think critically, but a separate and different *assessment* of critical thinking, and a separate but different *pedagogy* around critical thinking, then those separate and different methods, even if good individually, ultimately compete with one another.

But what if the *assessment* of thinking and the *method* for thinking are the *same thing*? What if the instrument for *assessing critical thinking* was the same *method* for doing critical thinking, and the same *pedagogy* for teaching critical thinking, and the same means of *assigning* critical thinking? Then, instead of experiencing different assignments, different assessments, and different methods, the students would only need to learn *one* thing. That "one" thing would be all of the things at the same time. And that's really what we mean by a critical thinking *holon*, and what we developed.

The nearly ubiquitous absence of the critical thinking *holon*, Dave and I discovered, is arguably the main reason many educators, including us initially, might work hard at trying to integrate critical thinking, as in by developing and using a critical thinking rubric, but nevertheless come up short with respect to positive outcomes. With the *holon* employed, students only need to learn *one* construct, and each part of that construct is all things. That's what makes it effective.

NEURO-BIOLOGICAL

In addition to being a *holon*, academia must tap the natural neuro-biological critical thinking hardwiring that evolution produced in *Homo sapiens*. Unfortunately, many critical thinking models fail to do that, which leads to critiques of critical thinking rubrics for relying on unclear definitions[194] and problematic subjectivity.[195] Those rubrics emerge, for instance, because a committee of educators may be tasked with developing a rubric, and each will impart their own potentially thoughtful but nevertheless idiosyncratic ideas for what critical thinking involves. The result is often a mish-mash of different terms and ideas, none of which are bad or wrong, per se, but they nevertheless might not form a cohesive *holon.*

Rather than devising a "hopeful" vision of critical thinking by committee, academia should predicate a thinking system on how *homo sapiens* evolved to think in the first place, which is what Dave and I developed. Such a system takes *homo sapiens'* natural neurobiological mechanisms for decision making and translates it into academia. Thus, the process students might use to think about their personal relationships, whether or not to attend class, how to advance in their careers, what to have for lunch, etc. becomes the same process they use to think critically about a business assignment or literary poem.

Rooting a thinking system in neuro-biological foundations taps students' innate, albeit raw abilities to think. It enables anyone using it to explain to their students that they do not need to teach the students *how* to think. They already think. Instead, they only need to help students translate their inborn thinking abilities into the academic context.

An analogy we use with students, educators, and execs is that, with limited exception, everyone can run. But to be a skilled runner requires taking that innate ability and training it in specific ways. By the same reasoning, students already possess the ability to think, but if they want to become better at it, they need to train that innate ability in specific ways.

I cannot overstate the difference between telling students that they need to learn how to think versus telling students that they are already thinking, and that we're going to help them do it better. The former can make them feel stupid. The latter makes them feel smart and empowered.

METACOGNITIVE

Once we have a *holon* rooted in neuro-biology, we also have something that's inherently metacognitive, "the simplest definition of [which] is that it is 'thinking about thinking'...but metacognition also involves knowing how to reflect and analyze thought, how to draw conclusions from that analysis, and how to put what has been learned into practice."[196] Arguably, "there would seem few more important accomplishments than people becoming aware of and reflective about their own thinking and able to monitor and manage the ways in which it is influenced by external sources, in both academic, work, and personal life settings."[197] Do you agree with that? Or not? Either way, do you really know what your brain did in order to make that determination? Are you self-aware of the mental process you used, your biases, your "logic"?

Few students if any, and very few *people* overall, are cognizant of the workings of their own thinking processes. But if we want students to think critically, then gaining that self-awareness is crucial. That's why effective critical thinking instruction goes *far* beyond just teaching students to identify logical fallacies in other people's arguments. It needs to make them self-aware of how they process their own ideas.

Metacognition, then, is a part of our holon as well, and with that system in place, metacognition isn't all too difficult. For example, one of the exercises Dave and I use is a *metalog*—a journal in which students apply our critical thinking system to decisions they make each day. Because our system overlays their natural thinking process, the decisions recorded in the log can be about *anything:* what they had for lunch, why they skipped a class, what they decided to share (or withhold) in a conversation with mom, etc. But it doesn't take very long, usually just a few days, before students stop just describing decisions they *already* made and start to become self-aware of how they *proactively* exercise the model while in the process of making new decisions. They become self-aware of their thinking as they do it.

INTERDISCIPLINARITY

Despite all the value of the *holon* above, it would cease being a *holon* if it also didn't work across the disciplines. If we want students to learn how to think critically, we need to build skills contiguously from course to course, grade level to grade level, and discipline to discipline. It might not seem groundbreaking to suggest that students will improve more readily if each course they take reinforces the same critical thinking skills, but remember that educators typically do not use clear standards for critical thinking in their own classes, much less consistently from class to class, grade to grade, and discipline to discipline.

Imagine, therefore, the utter disconnect students experience between one educator's expectations and the next. Students move from one (typically unspoken or ill-defined) concept of thinking in English 101 at 10:00am to an entirely different (yet still unspoken or ill-defined) concept of thinking in Introduction to U.S. History at 11:15 a.m. I don't think it is risky in this regard to ask you to reflect on your own academic past. How many times did you wonder, "What does *this* professor mean by "analyze"? What are *this* teacher's expectations *at all*?" These disparate, tacit, if not downright indecipherable shifts from course to course not only make it difficult for students to succeed in any one course, it certainly makes students struggle to develop any sustainable critical thinking skill overall.

Understanding the neuro-psychological burden of these disparities brings us to the term, *cognitive load*. In layperson terms, cognitive load refers to how much the brain can process at any one time, which, in thinking terms, isn't very much. If you've ever watched a child learning to ride a bike, you might have seen him ride it straight into a fence, tree, parked car, or curb. Why? Because when learning to ride a bike, the cognitive load becomes consumed by one thing and one thing only: not falling. With all the cognitive bandwidth on "don't fall," there's no bandwidth left, at first, for things such as steering or stopping. However, once their brains acclimate to not falling, the cognitive load for that function decreases. Then the brain can take on new cognitive loads, such as steering and stopping.

In stricter scientific terms, "[when] intrinsic cognitive load gradually decreases…a gradual increase of problem-solving demands is possible."[198] That's a fancier way of saying what Daniel Kahneman puts more plainly in *Thinking Fast and Slow*, "As you become skilled in a task, its demand for energy diminishes. Studies of the brain have shown that the pattern of activity associated with an action changes as skill increases, with fewer brain regions involved."[199]

In light of that relationship between increased skill and decreased cognitive load, consider the student who enters class number seventeen and is given the assignment to "analyze" *The Iliad*. That student needs to exert so much cognitive load figuring out what *this* professor means by analyze, how the professor grades, how to interpret the assignment, etc. etc. etc., that the student actually has less cognitive load for thinking and writing about *The Iliad* itself.

But don't take my word for it. There's ample evidence that students do not know what is expected of them. One study, for example, found that just 2 percent of students said that they were given "any handouts/handbooks, etc. explaining how to write" in their courses.[200] Another study found that about two-thirds of students said that different educators *in the same subject* required different things, and that half the time, those requirements aren't explained.[201] Adrift in such *confusion*, student brains devote high cognitive load to figuring out what's expected in each class, which only diminishes the energy they can devote to the real intellectual work we all want them to do: thinking about the *subjects*. In other words, they spend so much energy figuring out what the teacher wants in that assignment about *Moby Dick* that they don't spend nearly as much time as they could actually thinking about *Moby Dick*.

That confusion not only affects students, it also undermines how well educators can help students improve. Educators who nobly try to offer meaningful feedback for students on their essays often struggle to do so with any degree of effectiveness (whether they know it or not).[202,203,204] Because what is valued and how it is explained differs from course to course, "generic comments such as 'lacks synthesis of ideas' or 'performance was exemplary' can block further learning"[205] because students don't know how to decipher those phrases for *that* class (as opposed to in *all* of the other classes they've ever taken). It's not that educators don't *try* to explain, it's just that their use of comments such as "lacks synthesis" might conflict with, confuse, reject, etc. every other educator's use of that same phrase. Consequently, students don't know what any one educator means.

But what if that were different? What if, instead, the student entered a course already understanding the required critical thinking schema and the language of discourse around it? If that were the case, the student could devote all their cognitive load to *actually thinking about Moby Dick itself.*

That is the advantage of a critical thinking *holon* that works in all classes, in all disciplines, and at all levels. Once students learn the approach to critical thinking, they can apply it in any class. The content-specific knowledge might change, but *not* the expectation for how to intellectually engage that content. Students in this ecosystem no longer need to spend their cognitive load trying to figure out what the professor means by an assignment or how the professor will grade. Instead, the student can just go full-bore from the outset into thinking about the subject matter.

Imagine what a boon it is for *any* organization—academic, corporate, or otherwise—when every member becomes fluent in the same language and processes for critical thinking. Imagine how it facilitates, if not elevates and accelerates, the capacity to define and reason through problems. Such a system might be analogized to the brain's *myelin,* a lipid substance in the brain that increases the speed of communication neurons. It would be an accelerant to Yeats's kind of fire.

And think about what a blessing this is for faculty. Faculty in upper-level courses no longer need to explain what they expect or how students should go about doing it. They don't need to explain what they mean by analyzing or thinking critically. They don't need to explain how they'll grade papers. They don't need to come up with their own language for commenting on papers. Instead, students and educators alike become fluent in the same concept of critical thinking and the same language around how to discuss it.

At the university at which we worked, this approach produced strong outcomes. Thanks to many dedicated faculty, implementing this ecosystem model improved sophomore passing rates on our critical thinking portfolio from 8 percent in 2012 to about 50 percent in 2017. There are some important complexities and qualifications to those the gains, but there were powerful outcomes:

- Relative to papers that earned a C, papers earning a B+ or better showed 19.5 times the effort in engaging the quality of evidence.
- Out of 254 students surveyed, 95 percent who referenced our system's inforgraphic "very frequently" said it helped them become better critical thinkers.
- The pharmacy doctoral program saw critical thinking passing rates go from 28 percent for first year students to 80 percent for students in their second year.
- In a blind study, old papers that had been rated as exceptional for critical thinking under a previous system, papers that were typically by seniors, didn't even collectively meet the *minimal standard* achieved under our new system...by *sophomores*.

GENERATIVE

While all of the above is well and good, there's still one more thing critical thinking needs to accomplish for it to become meaningful and serve its most noble purposes. You see, *critical* thinking instruction often garners some well-deserved criticism because it connotes for many people, students especially, that critical thinking centers on being a critic. And that is *assuredly* where many students begin their journey into critical thinking: by spotting flaws and fallacies in other people's arguments. And that's fine. It is often necessary to understand where a discussion falls short if we are going to contribute something new to that discussion later on. But it's not enough to *just* be a critic, especially in a time where social media fosters *gotchaism*.

So, that's why it is essential that a critical thinking system is *generative*. The result of thinking cannot just be the identification of flaws but rather the *generation* of new ideas, ideas that might not make monumental contributions to intelligentsia, but ideas that at least attempt to move a discussion *forward*. Given the rapidly changing world in which we live, it is the generative force of thinking, not its *critic-al* one, that makes the "development of critical thinking skills…the most important reason for formal education…because the ability to think critically is essential for success in the contemporary world where the rate at which new knowledge is created is rapidly accelerating."[206]

Dave and I are hardly alone in calling for *generative* critical thinking. It just often falls under other terms, such as *creative thinking* or *divergent thinking*, and those are fine terms as well. The call for critical thinking to be generative is also becoming seen in the emergence of *innovation labs*, which are typically tech-based labs where students need to build something new, and *entrepreneurial* programs, where students conceive new startups.

However, innovation labs and entrepreneurial efforts, for all their value, miss part of the critical thinking equation. As Dave and I discuss on our podcast episode about "X-Labs," it's one thing for students to produce a new device but another thing for them to represent the thinking process that conceived it. We don't just need the *products* of innovation; we need to view and assess the innovation and thinking *process*. What if students produce a brilliant new thingamajig but it emerged from a series of fortunate accidents, random efforts, or even misunderstandings? The product would still be a good one, but we wouldn't necessarily want to trust them to design things in the future.

Not only that, no thingamajig will *ever* attend to some of the most important challenges facing our world. Racism, poverty, happiness, history, nursing research, etc. will never hinge on nor produce a *thing*. We need students who are adept in engaging the abstract. We need a process of training them for that and a means of measuring how well they contend with wicked problems.

The only solution to that, as advocated in this chapter, is a *critical thinking ecosystem,* a *holon* where educational institutions recognize that they need to become incubators that grow Little Brain into Big Brain—a large, powerful, mature critical thinker. After that, everything else becomes possible.

BEZOS'S MEMOS

Earlier, I mentioned that writing is an essential tool for teaching critical thinking, and it's time to return to that discussion. Writing is invaluable, and I'm not the only one to note it. In *Defense of a Liberal Education*, for example, Fareed Zakaria describes the extraordinary value Amazon's Jeff Bezos places on writing:

> *Bezos insists that his senior executives write memos, often as long six printed pages, and begins senior-management meetings with a period of quiet time, sometimes as long as thirty minutes, while everyone reads the "narratives" to themselves and makes notes on them…. Bezos said, "Full sentences are harder to write. They have verbs. The paragraphs have topic sentences. There is no way to write a six-page, narratively structured memo and not have clear thinking."*[207]

Having read my fair share of papers, I don't support Bezos's theory that "there is no way to write a six-page, narratively structured memo and have no clear thinking." I've seen plenty of vacuous six-page narratives. But his point about the importance and irreplaceable nature of writing is accurate, and that's not my opinion.

Thus, and in similar vein to Bezos's thinking, the College Board's National Commission on Writing in America's Schools and Colleges argued that when it comes to an effective education, a

> *commitment to writing, not simply among educators but also among policymakers and the general public, is one of the underdeveloped ingredients. If students are to make knowledge their own, they must struggle with the details, wrestle with the facts, and rework raw*

AMERICA'S CRITICAL THINKING CRISIS

information and dimly understood concepts into language they can communicate to someone else. In short, if students are to learn, they must write.[208]

Note here the emphasis that the College Board places on "making knowledge of their own." Writing, indeed, should hold that focus, because writing is uniquely equipped to do so.

As to why writing holds such irreplaceable power, the famous learning theorist, Lev Vygotsky, aptly noted that "written speech is considerably more conscious, and it is produced more deliberately, than oral speech." In similar advocacy of writing, the famous writing theorist, John Trimbur, emphasized the same point about how "cognition refers to the acquisition and application of knowledge through the complex mental processes...but the effective accomplishment of writing tasks over time requires even more. It calls upon metacognition, or the ability to perceive the very steps by which success occurs and to articulate the various qualities and components that contribute in significant ways to the production of successful writing."[209] And Bazerman and Tinburg, two contemporary writing theorists referencing more recent research, reiterated how writing uniquely serves as "a full act of the mind, drawing on the full resources of our nervous system, formulating communicative impulses into thoughts and words, and transcribing through the work of the fingers."[210]

Writing, therefore, possesses some unique properties when it comes to organizing and crystallizing thoughts. But Susan Langer, the renowned linguistic philosopher, goes one step further in capturing writing's true power. She not only writes that language grants us "the free, accomplished use of symbolism, [and] the record of articulate conceptual thinking," she extends the point to something much more important, which is that "without language there seems to be nothing like explicit thought whatsoever."[211] *Higher-order thinking arguably only happens through language, and, given what other researchers said above, writing more potently exercises that connection between language and thought than any other medium or process.* More specifically:

1. "Writing promotes explicitness, as the learner must make specific decisions about information
2. writing leads learners to make explicit connections between ideas…and organize them into a coherent whole.
3. The permanence of writing makes it easier to review, reexamine, connect, analyze, and critique ideas
4. It fosters a personal involvement with the target information, as the learner must decide how it will be treated
5. Writing helps learners think about what ideas mean, as they put them into their own written words."[212]

Writing's unique power to unify all those forces makes it our most needed tool in teaching and assessing critical thinking. What it does, in essence, is not just refine and record someone's thinking, but also allows us to *see* it.

Consider, for example, tasking a student with building a popsicle-stick bridge strong enough to hold a cinderblock. The student goes away and sometime later returns with a successfully strong bridge. Most people would conclude that the student engaged in successful critical thinking—the student solved the problem. But the conclusion that the student thought critically is flawed. Did the student just goof around and end up with a functional design? Was it haphazard trial and error? Did the student entirely misinterpret an engineering theory but stumble upon a working design nevertheless? Did the student copy a bridge design found on the internet? We don't know. The product of an intellectual act never demonstrates the process or quality of that intellectual act. Even if the student did, in fact, do something smart, can the student articulate what it was? Can the student replicate the smartness? Understanding the "smartness" of the product requires seeing the *thinking process* that generated that product, and writing is the best medium for that, period.

However, as I noted in Section I, writing's value depends on how expertly writing is employed, and the way educators use writing can commit the same fallacy as above—an emphasis on the product rather than the thinking process.* In academic writing, there are cognates to the popsicle-stick bridge. For example, there's evidence that educators grade papers with disproportional weight on the introduction relative to the conclusion or the body of the work.[213] The reasons are multifold but much pertains to the fact that the introduction sets the paper's thesis or idea, and, just like seeing a popsicle bridge, educators rate (or react to) that initial idea *without even seeing the thinking that substantiates it*.** A smart initial idea tends to generate a better grade than a lesser one. But educators not only should withhold judgement about the idea until they see the reasoning process for it, they should judge the reasoning process itself more than the final idea.

After all, how can we determine the thoughtfulness of an idea without seeing the thoughts? Even if the idea seems smart or even "right," it doesn't mean that the student came to it through a thoughtful process. Students often state theses that they never really develop, or they state interesting theses but then misinterpret sources, or they propose interesting theses that develop through false logic. In short, the good introduction with the interesting thesis might be followed by little or no substantive critical thinking.

In fact, *that's typically the case*. When we take faculty from varied academic institutions through their own students' writings and teach them methods for identifying definable moments of critical thinking, *they* almost invariably recognize that there are, at best, few moments of real critical thinking, even in the essays that their institution rated most highly. But I want to emphasize here that the absence

---

* Some educators will be familiar with the idea of "writing as a process" as part of the process movement that started in the early 1970s. My distinction between product and process here is a different one from that (though that's obviously important, as well).

** This is a natural *human* reaction, not just one of which educators are guilty. We *all* judge ideas on their face value at first. We have to consciously learn to not do that.

of thinking is *not* because their students lack intelligence. It's that, as this text has worked at length to describe, students lack direct instruction on how to think critically, and how to use their writing to articulate and amplify that thinking.

With one caveat (that will follow), writing should hold eminence in education. And compositionists, as well as writing instructors across the disciplines, should receive the strongest support and reverence. Institutions should rely almost exclusively on full-time faculty with dedicated training in the teaching of writing, and adjuncts, some of whom can be exceptional, should be screened carefully and selected meticulously.

But now the caveat. Writing only works for developing critical thinking when it is assessed with critical thinking in mind, arguably with a thinking-centered rubric. Or we could go one giant step further. What if instead of just presenting them with a critical thinking rubric, we presented them with a critical thinking *holon* that is a way of thinking, a way of teaching, a way of reading, a way of writing, and a way of assessing that is neurobiological and functions across all disciplines? If we did *that*, if we integrated the most powerful tool for critical thinking—writing—into a holistic system of critical thinking education, then consider the intellectual heights students could achieve.

Under that construct, writing and everyone who employs it across the disciplines would take the lead in the academy's transformation away from the ills of the previous section and toward the thinking-centered, and thinking-producing culture that I've shown to be possible. Writing isn't the only tool, but it could serve as the spark. And all of academia could feel its heat.

Remember, writing is already frequently employed in academia, so the question is not *if* it is used, but *how*. Its practices are deeply embedded, but, as Wittgenstein describes, "Getting hold of the difficulty deep down is what is hard. Because if it is grasped near the surface it simply remains the difficulty it was. It has to be pulled out by the roots; and that involves our beginning to think about these things in a new way. The change is as decisive as, for example, that from the alchemical to the chemical way of thinking. The new way of thinking is what is so hard to establish. Once the new way of thinking has been established, the old problems vanish; indeed, they become hard to recapture. For they go with our way of expressing ourselves and, if we clothe ourselves in a new form of expression, the old problems are discarded along with the old garment."

YEATS'S FIRE

My introduction to this book referenced my high school prom, where my peers and I gleefully shouted Rock Master Scott's lyrics about letting our school burn. In service of asking why students would want their school to burn, I have used (and arguably tortured) that moment. But I'm going to torture the metaphor even more. You see, I think something much deeper was happening there than students just cursing in front of their teachers. Upon clearer reflection, it wasn't a call for something to happen. It wasn't a desire to burn the school down.

It was a portent, and an ominous one at that.

The students of Sachem High School, who happened to be called, I kid you not, "The Flaming Arrows," were warning the world:

The school was *already* on fire.

Education *was already* burning.

That inferno assuredly didn't start with my senior class at Sachem High School in 1987 on Long Island. No, since the very start of modern U.S. education circa the Industrial Revolution, students have been warning educators that the school was on fire. All the students who resisted, who drooled on their desks during lectures, who were insubordinate, who daydreamed, who didn't care about The Hawley-Smoot Tariff Act, who couldn't wait for school to be out for summer, who just wanted to know what would be on the test, who didn't want to go back to school in the fall, who were brilliant philosophers never taught to philosophize, who longed to matter to the intellectual world, who laughed at school's absurdity in, to name just a few favorites from my era, *The Breakfast Club, Dead Poets Society, Ferris Beuller's Day Off,* and *Fast Times at Ridgemont High,* who desperately needed *help on their next date* but never got it—they *all* were warning us that education was burning.

How many cancers of this world haven't we cured because those naturally curious and critical minds that would have otherwise discovered cures were instead suffocated by memorizing and regurgitating what was already known? What would our world be today if education taught every child how to think critically about problems we never saw, toward solutions we don't know, with resources at which we might never even have glanced? What if educators were coaches of the intellectual mind, building through gritty drills its synaptic pathways for problem solving and social relevance? Instead of grading students on how many facts they know about questions we've already answered, what if we graded them on how well they could develop a critical idea of their own?

As I sit here today crafting the conclusion to this text, the Brazilian rainforest is burning, as is Australia, and California. Those infernos didn't ignite from deforestation as everyone claims. No, they caught fire from an ember that floated all the way from Sachem High School's roof in 1987, and from a million other embers from a million other academic institutions since the modern schooling era began.

We have an entire populous whose academic studies have been disconnected from their lives. Despite loving some of their teachers, maybe loving some subjects, and getting great jobs, they otherwise remained *indifferent* to a *confusing* education that never helped them on their next date. Is it such a wonder then that they feel disconnected from education? Is it any wonder at all that they believe that intellectual study doesn't matter to the world? Is it strange even in the least that those for whom academic learning never helped them on their next date also didn't listen when the academics and scientists warned that climate change would someday burn the rainforests? Why should they believe us now when we'd failed for so long to make learning relevant to their world?

I hope it is easy to conclude now that education must change so that the children of today will value those highly educated experts who warn them of the next crisis. More importantly, I hope it is clear that it must change so that they will become those experts, millions and millions of them, experts in thinking and solving and ideating and persisting and philosophizing, experts who excel not in understanding what is known but in understanding what *isn't*.

To get there, I recommend that we follow Jacques Berlinerblau's call in *Campus Confidential* for every campus to have a "Dean of Pedagogy. Her powers would be immense—'dangerously uncircumscribed,' complains the Faculty Senate. Her job would be to scrutinize the classroom experience on her campus...in my reveries, the Dean of Pedagogy is authorized to completely fuck up [faculty] shit, by which I mean...tenure prospects or...reappointment. Are you neglecting your classes? Do you spend your office hours hidden in a library study carrel munching on granola bars? Did you hand back your first graded assignment a week before class ended? Did you last read the novel you lectured on today around the time Bush invaded Iraq (and by this, I mean H.W., naturally)? If so, The Dean of Pedagogy will take you *down!*"

Higher education could easily reallocate spending from costly dorms and smart classrooms to far-cheaper faculty training in the *teaching of critical thinking*. New faculty, who in higher education come with no training in how to teach, might be required to spend their first semester, or first *year*, shadowing master educators before even being allowed to teach a course of their own. (Would you go to a surgeon who has not watched experienced surgeons performing your surgery? Would you want the new lawyer who never shadowed his or her seniors in court? You would not trust your body or your trial to such people, and yet we entrust our students' minds to professors who, despite their noble intentions and wide range of skills, might never have been taught how to teach.) Education can become something very, very different from what it was for the students of Sachem High School, and from what it is today.

And that returns us, at last, to our battle between Rock Master Scott and William Butler Yeats. Rock Master Scott's fire is burning the world from Australia to California. But Yeats's fire is achievable if we want it. Education should be "the lighting of a fire" and it should ignite student minds with brilliant ideas, pyres of failures, sparks of success, and blazing solutions. That's how it *should* burn.

But the nut of all of this is that *education is going to burn one way or another*. It's burning up the rainforests right now. And on its current course, more of the world will "burn" soon one way or another.

Fortunately, we can still choose how it burns moving forward. We do it wrong and Rock Master Scott's fire wins; education burns itself to a smoldering ash heap, taking many of us and our children down with it. Or we do it right and ignite millions of young minds such that they burn with a powerful luminescence that lights the darkness of intellectual oblivion. Either way, whether it be watching the existing system burn itself down or, I hope, watching the glorious illumination of our collective future, I say, and I hope you say...

> *We don't need no water*
> *Let the motherfucker burn.*
> *Burn, motherfucker.*
> *Burn.*

For inquiries about speaking engagements, educational or corporate consulting, or just for comments and questions, please reach me at *stevenpearlman@gmail.com*.

ENDNOTES

1   Pinker, S. (2019). *Enlightenment Now.* Penguin. p. 8.

2   Koenig, M. & Tiberius, V. (2017). Can children save us from the" fake news" epidemic? *NBC News.* https://www.nbcnews.com/think/opinion/can-children-save-us-fake-news-epidemic-ncna830316

3   Willingham, D. T. (2007). Critical Thinking: Why Is It So Hard to Teach? *American Educator.*

4   Butler, H.A., Pentoney, C., and Bong, M.P. (2016). Predicting real-world outcomes: Critical thinking ability is a better predictor of real life decisions than intelligence. *Thinking Skills and Creativity, 25, 38–46.*

5   Hart Research Associates. (2013). It Takes More Than a Major: Employer Priorities for College Learning and Student Success. *Association of American Colleges & Universities.*

6   Hart Research Associates. (2018). Fulfilling the American dream: Liberal education and the future of work. *Association of American Colleges and Universities.*

7   Bouygues, H. L. (2018). *The State of Critical Thinking: A New Look at Reasoning at Home, School, and Work. Reboot*

8   DeAngelo, L., Hurtado, S., Pryor, J. H., Kelly, K. R., Santos, J. L., & Korn, W. S. (2009). *The American college teacher: National norms for the 2007–2008 HERI faculty survey.* Los Angeles, CA: Higher Education Research Institute, p. 3.

9   Strang, T. (2014). The importance of teaching critical thinking. Retrieved from: https:// blog.cengage.com/importance-teaching-critical-thinking/

10 *State of Critical Thinking.* MindEdge

11 Bouygues, H. L. (2018). The state of critical thinking. Reboot: Elevating Critical Thinking.

12 Breslin, F. (2016). Why public schools don't teach critical thinking—Part 1. *Huffington Post.*

13 Berrett, D. (2016). If skills are the new canon, are colleges teaching them? *The Chronicle of Higher Education.*

14 Huber, C.R., Kuncel, N.R. (2017). Does college teach critical thinking: A meta-analysis. *Review of Educational Research, 86*(2), 431–468.

15 Possin, K. (2016). Commentary on "Why not teach critical thinking" by B. Hamby. *OSSA Conference Archive.* 60

16 Poh, M., Swenson, N.C., and Picard, R.W. (2010). A wearable sense for unobtrusive, long-term assessment of electrodermal activity. *IEEE Transactions on Biomedical Engineering, 57*(5), 1243–1252.

17 Noel-Levitz Employer Satisfaction Survey (2010). As cited in Jenkins, R. (2017). Why college graduates still can't think. *The James G. Martin Center for Academic Renewal.* https://www.jamesgmartin.center/2017/03/college-graduates-still-cant-think/

18 Learning our lesson: Review of Quality Teaching in Higher Education. (2016). *Organisation for Economic Co-operation and Development.*

19 Disciplinary distribution of bachelor's degrees in the humanities. (2015). *American Academy of Arts & Sciences.* https://humanitiesindicators.org/content/indicatordoc.aspx?i=34

20 Belkin, D. (2017). Liberal arts college, in fight for survival, focus on job skills. *The Wall Street Journal.*

21 College Salary Report. (2008). *Payscale.* http://www.payscale.com/best-colleges/salary-report.asp

22 Hartley, S. (2018). *The fuzzy and the techie: Why the liberal arts will rule the world.* Mariner. p. 28.

23 Hartley, S. (2018). *The fuzzy and the techie: Why the liberal arts will rule the world.* Mariner. p. 5–6.

24 Roth, M.S. (2015). *Beyond the university: Why liberal education matters.* Yale. p. 3

25 Hartley, S. (2018). *The fuzzy and the techie: Why the liberal arts will rule the world.* Mariner. p. 27.

26 Tsui, L. (1999). Courses and instruction affecting critical thinking. *Research in Higher Education, 40*(2), 185–200.

27 O'Rourke, J., Main, S., and Cooper, M. (2014). Student perceptions of online interactive versus traditional lectures; or how I managed not to fall asleep with my eyes open. *MERLOT Journal of Online Learning and Teaching, 10*(3), 405–419.

28 Zull, J.E. (2002). *The art of changing the brain.* Stylus. p. 149.

29 Zull, J.E. (2002). *The art of changing the brain.* Stylus. p. 40

30   Zull, J.E. (2002). *The art of changing the brain*. Stylus. p. 41

31   Poldrack, R.A., Halchenko, Y., & Hanson, S.J. (2009). Decoding the large-scale structure of brain function by classifying mental states across individual. *Psychological Science, 20*(11), 1364–1372.

32   Szpunar, K.K., Kahn, N.Y, Schacter, D.L. (2013). Interpolated memory tests reduce mind wandering and improve learning of online lectures. *Proceedings of the National Academy of Sciences*, 110(16), 6313-6317.

33   Bonawitz, E. et al. (2011). The double-edged sword of pedagogy: Instruction limits spontaneous exploration of discovery. *Cognition, 120*(3), 322–330.

34   Willis, J. (2014). Neuroscience reveals that boredom hurts. *Student learning: Engagement & Motivation*, 28–32.

35   Willis, J. (2014). Neuroscience reveals that boredom hurts. *Student learning: Engagement & Motivation*, 28–32.

36   Evrard, M.R., and Ludvik, M.J.B (2016). Unpacking neuroplasticity and neurogenesis. In Ludvic, M.J.B. (Ed.), *The Neuroscience of Learning and Development: Enhancing Creativity, Compassion, Critical Thinking, and Peace in Higher Education* (pp. 54–72). Sterling, VA: Stylus.

37   Willis, J. (2014). Neuroscience reveals that boredom hurts. *Student learning: Engagement & Motivation*, 28–32.

38   Willis, J. (2014). Neuroscience reveals that boredom hurts. *Student learning: Engagement & Motivation*, 28–32.

39   Willis, J. (2014). Neuroscience reveals that boredom hurts. *Student learning: Engagement & Motivation*, 28–32.

40   Deslauriers, L., McCarty, L.S., Miller, K., Callaghan, K., and Kestin, G. (2019). Measuring actual learning versus feeling of learning in response to being actively engaged in the classroom. *Proceedings of the National Academy of Sciences, 116*(39), 19251–19257. www.pnas.org/cgi/doi/10.1073/pnas.1821936116

41   Deslauriers, L., McCarty, L.S., Miller, K., Callaghan, K., and Kestin, G. (2019). Measuring actual learning versus feeling of learning in response to being actively engaged in the classroom. *Proceedings of the National Academy of Sciences, 116*(39), 19251–19257. www.pnas.org/cgi/doi/10.1073/pnas.1821936116 www.pnas.org/cgi/doi/10.1073/pnas.1821936116

42 Deslauriers, L., McCarty, L.S., Miller, K., Callaghan, K., and Kestin, G. (2019). Measuring actual learning versus feeling of learning in response to being actively engaged in the classroom. *Proceedings of the National Academy of Sciences, 116*(39), 19251–19257. www.pnas.org/cgi/doi/10.1073/pnas.1821936116 www.pnas.org/cgi/doi/10.1073/pnas.1821936116

43 Tiruneh, D.T., Verburgh, A., & Elen, J. (2014). Effectiveness of critical thinking instruction in higher education: A systematic review of intervention studies. *Higher Education Studies, 4*(1), 1–17.

44 Tiruneh, D.T., Verburgh, A., & Elen, J. (2014). Effectiveness of critical thinking instruction in higher education: A systematic review of intervention studies. *Higher Education Studies, 4*(1), 1–17.

45 Nicholas, M.C., & Raider-Roth, M. (2016). A hopeful pedagogy to critical thinking. *International Journal for the Scholarship of Teaching and Learning, 10*(2), 1–10.

46 Laird, T.F.L., Seifert, T.A., Pascarella, E.T., Mayhew, M.J., & Blaich, C.F. (2014). Deeply affecting first-year students' thinking: Deep approaches to learning and the three dimensions of cognitive development. *The Journal of Higher Education, 85*(3), 402–432.

47 Choy, S.C., Cheah, P.K. (2009). Teacher perceptions of critical thinking among students and its influence on higher education. *International Journal of Teaching and Learning in Higher Education, 20*(2), 198–206.

48 Johnson, R.H. & Blair, J.A. (2012). Teaching the dog's breakfast: Some dangers and how to deal with them. *American Association of Physics Teachers* conference.

49 Blikstein, P. as referenced in Kantrowitz, B. (2014). Scientists bring new rigor to education research. *Scientific American.* https://www.scientificamerican.com/article/scientists-bring-new-rigor-to-education-research/

50 Hartley, S. (2018). *The fuzzy and the techie: Why the liberal arts will rule the world.* Mariner.

51 Tsui, L. (2002). Fostering critical thinking through effective pedagogy: Evidence from four institutional case studies. *The Journal of Higher Education, 73*(6), 740–763.

52 Zakaria, F. (2016). *In Defense of a Liberal Education.* W. W. Norton. 73.

53 Condon, W. & Kelly-Riley, D. Assessing and teaching what we value: The relationship between college-level writing and critical thinking abilities. *Assessing Writing, 9,* 56–75.

54 Gillespie, A., Graham, S., Kiuhara, S., and Hebert, M. (2014). High school teachers use of writing to support students' learning: a national survey. *Reading and Writing, 27,* 1043–1072.

55 Graham, S., & Hebert, M. (2011). Writing-to-read: A meta-analysis of the impact of writing and writing instruction on reading. Harvard Educational Review, 81, 710–744.

56 Applebee, A.N. and Langer, J.A. (2011). *English Journal, 100*(6), 14–27.

57 Schmoker, M. (2018). Demystifying writing, transforming education. *Educational Leadership, 75*(7), 22–27.

58 National Commission on Writing. (2003, April). *The neglected "r": The need for a writing revolution.* New York: The College Board.

59 Melzer, D. (2014). *Assignments across the curriculum: A national study of college writing.* Utah State University.

60 Portanova, P., Rifenburg, J.M., & Roen, D. (2017). Introduction. In Portanova, P., Rifenburg, J.M., & Roen, D. (Ed.), *Contemporary perspectives on cognition and writing,* 3–18. WAC Clearinghouse.

61 Meade, M. (2017). Seeing is believing: Re-presentation, cognition, and transfer in writing classes. In Portanova, P., Rifenburg, J.M., & Roen, D. (Ed.), *Contemporary perspectives on cognition and writing,* 231–246. WAC Clearinghouse.

62 National Cense of Writing. (2018). Swarthmore. https://writingcensus. swarthmore.edu

63 Anderson, P., Anson, C.M., Gonyea, R.M., & Paine, C. (2015). The contributions of writing to learning and development: Results from a large-scale multi-institutional study. *Research in the Teaching of English, 50*(2), 199–235.

64 Jamieson, S. (2014). Reading and Engaging Sources: What students' use of sources reveals about advanced reading skills. *Across the Disciplines, 10*(4).

65 Howard, Rebecca Moore. (1993). A Plagiarism pentimento. *Journal of Teaching Writing, 11*(2), 233–46.

66 Bazerman, C. (2017). The psychology of writing situated within social action: An empirical and theoretical program. In Portanova, P., Rifenburg, J.M., & Roen, D. (Ed.), *Contemporary perspectives on cognition and writing,* 21–38. WAC Clearinghouse.

67 Bazerman, C. (2017). The psychology of writing situated within social action: An empirical and theoretical program. In Portanova, P., Rifenburg, J.M., & Roen, D. (Ed.), *Contemporary perspectives on cognition and writing,* 21–38. WAC Clearinghouse.

[68] Cited in Tversky, B. (2019). *Mind in Motion*. Basic. 47.

[69] Bacon, D. R., & Stewart, K. A. (2006). How fast do students forget what they learn in consumer behavior? A longitudinal study. *Journal of Marketing Education, 28*(3), 181-192.

[70] Engel, S. (2015). *The Hungry Mind*. Harvard.

[71] Gibbs, G. (1992) *Improving the Quality of Student Learning*. Bristol: Technical and Educational Services.

[72] Poldrack, R.A., Halchenko, Y., & Hanson, S.J. (2009). Decoding the large-scale structure of brain function by classifying mental states across individual. *Psychological Science, 20*(11), 1364–1372.

[73] Anderson, P., Anson, C.M., Gonyea, R.M., & Paine, C. (2015). The contributions of writing to learning and development: Results from a large-scale multi-institutional study. *Research in the Teaching of English, 50*(2), 199–235.

[74] Kolowich, S. (2014). Confuse students to help them learn. *The Chronicle of Higher Education*. https://www.chronicle.com/article/Confuse-Students-to-Help-Them/148385

[75] Kolowich, S. (2014). Confuse students to help them learn. *The Chronicle of Higher Education*. https://www.chronicle.com/article/Confuse-Students-to-Help-Them/148385

[76] Kolowich, S. (2014). Confuse students to help them learn. *The Chronicle of Higher Education*. https://www.chronicle.com/article/Confuse-Students-to-Help-Them/148385.

[77] Caine, R.N. & Caine, G. (2011). *Natural learning for a connected world: Education, technology, and the human brain*. Teachers College. 72.

[78] Caine, R.N. & Caine, G. (2011). *Natural learning for a connected world: Education, technology, and the human brain*. Teachers College. 71.

[79] Singleton-Jackson, J.A., Jackson, D.L., & Reinhardt, J. (2010). Students as consumers of knowledge: Are they buying what we're selling? *Innovative Higher Education, 35*, 343–358.

[80] Breslin, F. (2016). Why public schools don't teach critical thinking—Part 1. *Huffington Post*.

[81] Coch, D. (2010). Constructing a reading brain. In Sousa, D.A. (Ed.) *Mind, Brain, & Education, 139–163*. Solution Tree. 151.

[82] Singleton-Jackson, J.A., Jackson, D.L., & Reinhardt, J. (2010). Students as consumers of knowledge: Are they buying what we're selling? *Innovative Higher Education, 35*, 343–358.

[83] McCabe, J., & Powell, B. (2004). "In my class? No." Professors accounts of grade inflation. In Becker, W.E. and M. L. Andrews, M.L. (Ed.), *The Scholarship of Teaching and Learning in Higher Education: Contributions of Research Universities.* Indiana University.

[84] Rojstaczer, S., &. Healy, C. (2012). Where A is ordinary: The evolution of American college and university grading, 1940–2009. *Teachers College Record, 14,* 1–23.

[85] Thomas, B., & Wasley, P. (2008). Just say 'A': Grading inflation undergoes reality check. *Chronicle of Higher Education, 55(2).*

[86] Carter, MJ and Lara, PY. (2016). Grade inflation in higher education: Is the end in sight. *Academic Questions, 29,* 346–353.

[87] Jaschik, S. (2017). High school grades: Higher and higher. *Inside Higher Ed.*

[88] Cooper, C. (2017). Why GPAs are rising while SAT scores fall. *PrepExpert.*

[89] Cooper, C. (2017). Why GPAs are rising while SAT scores fall. *PrepExpert.*

[90] Betts, J., & Grogger, J. (2000). The impact of grading standards on student achievement, educational attainment, and entry-level earnings. *National Bureau of Economic Research, 7875, 1–31.*

[91] Malkiel, N. *Report to Faculty on Grading Proposals.* Princeton. www.princeton.edu/%7eodoc/grading_ proposals/, memo, 2004.

[92] Babock, P. (2010). Real costs of nominal grade inflation? New evidence from student course evaluations. *Economic Inquiry,* 48(4), 983–996.

[93] Greenberger, E., Lessard, J., Chuansheng, C., & Farrugia, S. (2008). Self-entitled college students: Contributions of personality, parenting, and motivational Factors. *Journal of Youth & Adolescence, 37,* 1193–1204.

[94] Singleton-Jackson, J.A., Jackson, D.L., & Reinhardt, J. (2010). Students as consumers of knowledge: Are they buying what we're selling? *Innovative Higher Education, 35,* 343–358.

[95] Twenge, J.M., & Campbell, W. K. (2009). *The narcissism epidemic: Living in the age of entitlement.* Simon & Schuster.

[96] Luckett, M., Trocchia, P. J., Joel, M. N., & Marlin, D. (2017). A typology of students based on academic entitlement. *Journal of Education for Business, 92(2),* 96–102.

[97] Luckett, M., Trocchia, P. J., Joel, M. N., & Marlin, D. (2017). A typology of students based on academic entitlement. *Journal of Education for Business, 92(2),* 96–102.

98   Fingerman, K. L., Cheng, Y. P, Wesselmann, E. D., Zarit, S., Furstenberg, F., & Birditt, K. S. (2012). Helicopter parents and landing pad kids: Intense parental support of grown children. *Journal of Marriage and Family, 74*, 880–896.

99   Greenberger, E., Lessard, J., Chuansheng, C., & Farrugia, S. (2008). Self-entitled college students: Contributions of personality, parenting, and motivational Factors. *Journal of Youth & Adolescence, 37*, 1193–1204

100   Valsan, C. and Sproule, R. (2008). The invisible hands behind the student evaluation of teaching: The rise of the managerial elite in the governance of higher education. *Journal of Economic Issues*, 42(4), 939–958.

101   McPherson, M. A., & Jewell, R. T. (2007). Leveling the playing field: should student evaluation scores be adjusted? Social Science Quarterly (Blackwell Publishing Limited), 88, 868–881.

102   Valsan, C. and Sproule, R. (2008). The invisible hands behind the student evaluation of teaching: The rise of the managerial elite in the governance of higher education. *Journal of Economic Issues*, 42(4), 939–958.

103   Trathern, M. Improving Ratings. *Audit in the British University System European Review*, 5, 305–321.

104   Bruff, D. *Agile Learning*. As cited in, Davidson, C.N. (2017). *The New Education: How to Revolutionize the University to Prepare Students for a World in Flux*. Basic Books.

105   Gentry, J. (2011). Radical change in facult and student evaluation: A justifiable heresy? *Administrative Issues Journal, 1*.

106   Allen, I. E., & Seaman, J. (2013). Changing course: Ten years of tracking online education in the United States. *Babson Survey Research Group, Pearson Publishers and Sloan Foundation*.

107   Ginder, S.A., Kelly-Reid, J.E., and Mann, F.B. (2018). *Enrollment and Employees in Postsecondary Institutions, Fall 2017; and Financial Statistics and Academic Libraries, Fiscal Year 2017: First Look (Provisional Data)* (NCES 2019- 021rev). U.S. Department of Education. Washington, DC: National Center for Education Statistics. http://nces.ed.gov/pubsearch.

108   Allen, I. E., & Seaman, J. (2013). Changing course: Ten years of tracking online education in the United States. *Babson Survey Research Group, Pearson Publishers and Sloan Foundation*.

109   Katz, Y. J. & Yablon, Y. B. (2002). Who is afraid of university internet courses? *Educational Media International, 39*, 1, 69–73.

[110] Stack, S. (2015) Learning outcomes in an online versus traditional course. *International Journal for the Scholarship of Teaching and Learning, 9*(1), 1–18.

[111] Cavanaugh, J.K., & Jacquemin, S.J. (2015). A large sample comparison of grade based student learning outcomes in line versus face-to-face courses. *Online Learning, 19*(2), 25–32.

[112] Moten, J. Jr., Fitterer, A., Brazier, E., Leonard, J. & Brown, A. (2013). Examining online college cyber cheating methods and prevention measures. *The Electronic Journal of e-Learning, 11*, 139–146.

[113] Hart, C., Friedmann, E., and Hill, M. (2018). Online course-taking and student outcomes in California community colleges. *Education Finance and Policy, 13*(1), 42–71.

[114] Callister, R. R., Love, M. S. (2016). A comparison of learning outcomes in skills-based courses: Online versus face-to-face formats. *Decision Sciences Journal of Innovative Education, 14*(2), 243–256.

[115] Dennis, JK. (2003). Problem-based learning in online versus face-to-face environments. *Education for Health* 16(2), 198–209.

[116] Dennis, JK. (2003). Problem-based learning in online versus face-to-face environments. *Education for Health* 16(2), 198–209.

[117] Grygiel, J. (2012). The MOOC fraud. *The American Interest. https://www.the-american-interest.com/2013/12/19/the-mooc-fraud/*

[118] Pearson student mobile device survey. National Report: College Students. (2015). *Pearson.* https://www.pearsoned.com/wp-content/uploads/2015-Pearson-Student-Mobile-Device-Survey-College.pdf

[119] Ravizza, S.M., Uitvlugt, M.G., & Fenn, K.M. (2017). Logged in and Zoned Out. *Psychological Science, 28*(2), 171–180.

[120] Ravizza, S.M., Uitvlugt, M.G., & Fenn, K.M. (2017). Logged in and Zoned Out. *Psychological Science, 28*(2), 171–180.

[121] Brooks, D.C., Pomerantz, J. (2017). ECAR study of undergraduate students and information technology, 2017. Research Report. *ECAR.*

[122] Zhou, Y., Lin, F., Du, Y., Qin, L., Zhao, Z., Xu, J., & Lei, H. Gray matter abnormalities in internet addiction: A Voxel-based morphometry study. *European Journal of Radiology* 79(1), 92–95.

[123] Yuan, K., Cheng, P., Dong, T., Bi, Y., Xing, L., Yu, D., Zhao, L., Dong, M., Deneen, K.M., Liu, Y., Qin, W. & Tian, J. (2013). Cortical thickness abnormalities in late adolescence with online gaming addiction. Abnormalities in Late Adolescence with Onlien Gaming Addiction." *PloS ONE 8*(1).

[124] Weng, C., Qian, R., Fu, X., Lin, B., Han, X., Niu, C., Want, Y. (2013). Gray matter and white matter abnormalities in online game addiction. *European Journal of Radiology 82*(8), 1308–1312.

[125] Wolf, M. (2018). Skim reading is the new normal. The effect on society is profound. *The Guardian*. https://www.theguardian.com/commentisfree/2018/aug/25/skim-reading-new-normal-maryanne-wolf

[126] Horowitz-Kraus, T. & Hutton, J.S. (2017). Brain connectivity in children is increased by the time they spend reading books and decreased by the length of exposure to screen-based media. ACTA Pediatrica, 107(4).

[127] Craig, R. J., & Amernic, J. H. (2006). PowerPoint presentation technology and the dynamics of teaching. *Innovation in Higher Education, 31*, 147–160.

[128] Van Jole, F. (2000). Het PowerPoint denken. As quoted in Craig, R. J., & Amernic, J. H. (2006). PowerPoint presentation technology and the dynamics of teaching. *Innovation in Higher Education, 31*, 147–160.

[129] Isseks, M. (2011). How PowerPoint is killing education. *Education Leadership, 68*(5), 74–76.

[130] Isseks, M. (2011). How PowerPoint is killing education. *Education Leadership, 68*(5), 74–76.

[131] Tzu, S. (2017) *The Art of War*. Translated by Lionel Giles. Quorto.

[132] Chambliss, D.F., & Takacs, C.G. (2014). *How College Works*. Harvard UP.

[133] Teneva, M. (2019). Dynamics in diagnosing the quality of the good teacher. *Trakia Journal of Sciences, 2*, 101–106.

[134] Beishuzen, J. J., Hof, E., van Putten, C.M., Bouwmeester, S., & Asscher, J. J. (2001). Students' and teachers' cognitions about good teachers. *British Journal of Educational Psychology, 71*(2), 185–201.

[135] Lizzio, A., & Wilson, K. (2008). Feedback on assessment: Students' perceptions of quality and effectiveness. *Assessment & Evaluation in Higher Education, 33*(3), 263–275.

[136] Duckworth, A. Grit: Perseverance and passion for long-term goals. *Journal of Personality and Social Psychology, 92*(6), 1087–1101.

[137] Crede, M., Tynan, M.C., & Harms, P.D. (2017). Much ado about grit: A meta-analytic synthesis of the grit literature. *Journal of Personality and Social Psychology, 113*(3), 492–511.

[138] Chang, W. (2014). Grit and academic performance: Is being grittier better? (Unpublished doctoral dissertation). University of Miami, Mi- ami, FL.

[139] Crede, M., Tynan, M.C., & Harms, P.D. (2017). Much ado about grit: A meta-analytic synthesis of the grit literature. *Journal of Personality and Social Psychology*, 113(3), 492–511.

[140] Wolfe, R.N., & Johnson, S.D. (1995). Personality as a predictor of college performance. *Educational and Psychological Measurement, 55,* 177–185.

[141] Rimfield, K., Kovas, Y., Dale, P.S., & Plomin, R. (2016). True grit and genetics: Predicting academic achievement from personality. *Journal of Personality and Social Psychology, 111*(5), 780–789.

[142] Rimfield, K., Kovas, Y., Dale, P.S., & Plomin, R. (2016). True grit and genetics: Predicting academic achievement from personality. *Journal of Personality and Social Psychology, 111*(5), 780–789.

[143] Robbins, S.B., Lauver, K., Le, H., Davis, D., Langley, R., & Carlstrom, A. (2004). Do psychosocial and study skills factors predict college outcomes? A mea-analysis. *Psychological Bulletin, 130,* 261–288.

[144] Muenks, K., Wigfield, A., Yang, J.S., and O'Neal, R.. (2016). How true is grit? Its relations to high school and college students' personality characteristics, self-regulation, engagement, and achievement. *Journal of Educational Psychology, 109*(5), 599–620.

[145] Bazelais, P., Lemay, D.J., and Doleck, T. (2016). How does grit impact college students' academic performance in science? *European Journal of Science and Mathematics Education, 4*(1), 33–43.

[146] Hoerr, T.R. (2012). *Fostering Grit: How do I prepare my students for real the real world?* ASCD.

[147] Savery, R.J. (2006). Overview of problem-based learning: Definitions and distinctions. *Interdisciplinary Journal of problem-based learning, 1*(1), 9–20.

[148] Nappi, J.S. (2017). The importance of questioning in developing critical thinking skills. *Delta Kappa Gamma Bulletin,* 84(1), 30–41.

[149] Mallow, J. V. (2001). Student group project work: A pioneering experiment in interactive engagement. Journal of Science Education and Technology, 10(2), 105-113.

[150] Chouinard, M.M. (2007). Children's questions: A mechanism for cognitive development. *Monographs of the Society for Research in Child Development, 72,* 1–129.

[151] Gruber, M.J., Gelman, B.D., Ranganath, C. (2014). States of curiosity modulate hippocampus-dependent learning via the dopaminergic circuit. *Neuron, 84*(2), 486–496.

152 Dochy, F., Mien, S., Van den Bossche, P., Gijbels, D. (2003). Effects of problem-based learning: A meta-analysis. *Learning and Instruction, 13*(5), 533–568.

153 Strobel, J., & van Barneveld, A. (2009). When is PBL more effective? A meta-synthesis of meta-analyses comparing PBL to conventional classrooms. *Interdisciplinary Journal of Problem-based Learning, 3*(1), 44–58.

154 Hmelo-Silver, C.E. (2004). Problem-based learning: What and how do students learn? *Educational Psychology Review, 16*(3), 235–266.

155 Bate, E., Hommes, J., Duvivier, R., and Taylor, D.C.M. (2014). Problem-based learning (PBL): Getting the most out of your students—Their roles and responsibilities: AMEE Guide No. 84. *Medical Teacher*, 36, 1–12.

156 Rotgants, J. I., & Schmidt, H. G. (2011). Cognitive engagement in the problem-based learning classroom. *Adv in Health Sci Educ*, 16, 465–479.

157 Barak, M., & Dori, Y.J. (2009). Enhancing higher order thinking skills among inservice science teachers via embedded assessment. *Journal of Science Teacher Education, 20*(5), 459–474.

158 Bate, E., Hommes, J., Duvivier, R., and Taylor, D.C.M. (2014). Problem-based learning (PBL): Getting the most out of your students—Their roles and responsibilities: AMEE Guide No. 84. *Medical Teacher*, 36, 1–12.

159 Major, C.H., & Palmer, B. (2006). Reshaping teaching and learning: The transformation of faculty pedagogical content knowledge. *Journal of Higher Education, 51*, 619–647.

160 Dochy, F., Mien, S., Van den Bossche, P., Gijbels, D. (2003). Effects of problem-based learning: A meta-analysis. *Learning and Instruction, 13*(5), 533–568.

161 Kwon, Y., Lee, J, Shin, D, and Jeong, J. (2009). Changes in brain activation induced by the training of hypothesis generation skills: An fMRI study. *Brain and Cognition, 69*(2), 391–397.

162 Kwon, Y., Lee, J, Shin, D, and Jeong, J. (2009). Changes in brain activation induced by the training of hypothesis generation skills: An fMRI study. *Brain and Cognition, 69*(2), 391–397.

163 Bashant, J. (2014). Developing grit in our students: Why grit is such a desirable trait, and practical strategies for teachers and schools. *Journal of Leadership and Instruction, 13*(2), 14–17.

164 Tsui, L. (2006). Cultivating critical thinking: Insights from an elite liberal arts college. *The Journal of General Education, 55*(2), 200–227.

[165] Wenger, E. (1998). *Communities of practice: Learning, meaning and identity.* Cambridge University Press.

[166] Wenger, E. (1998). *Communities of practice: Learning, meaning and identity.* Cambridge University Press.

[167] Jamieson, J. P., Mendes, W. B., Blackstock, E., & Schmader, T. (2010). Turning the knots in your stomach into bows: Reappraising arousal improves performance on the GRE. Journal of Experimen- tal Social Psychology, 46, 208–212.

[168] Mendes, W. B., Blascovich, J., Hunter, S. B., Lickel, B., & Jost, J. T. (2007). Threatened by the unexpected: physiological responses during social interactions with expectancy-violating partners. Journal of personality and social psychology, 92, 698.

[169] Lyons, I. M., & Beilock, S. L. (2012). When math hurts: Math anxiety predicts pain network activation in anticipation of doing math. PloS One, 7, e48076.

[170] Ludvik, M.J.B, Evrar, M.R., and Goldin, P. (2016). Strategies that intentionally change the brain. In Ludvic, M.J.B. (Ed.), *The Neuroscience of Learning and Development: Enhancing Creativity, Compassion, Critical Thinking, and Peace in Higher Education* (pp. 73–98). Stylus.

[171] Brown, P.C., Roediger III, H.L., and McDaniel, M.A. (2014). *Make it Stick: The Science of Successful Learning.* Harvard.

[172] Immordino-Yang, M.H., & Faeth, M. The role of emotion and skilled intuition in learning. In Sousa, D.A. (Ed.) *Mind, Brain, & Education, 69–84.* Solution Tree.

[173] Van Duijuvenoorde, A.C.K., Zanolie, K., Rombouts, S.A.R.B., Raijmakers, M.E.J., & Crone, E.A. (2008). Evaluating the negative or valuing the positive? Neural mechanisms supporting feedback-based learning across development. *The Journal of Neuroscience, 28*(38), 9495–9503.

[174] Collins, S. (2016). *The Neuroscience of Learning and Development.* Kogen Page Limited. 127.

[175] Morales, T. M., Bang, E., & Andre, T. (2013). A one-year case study: Understanding the rich potential of project-based learning in a virtual reality class for high school students. Journal of Science, Education, and Technology, 22, 791–806.

[176] Ambrose, S.A., Bridges, M.W., Mihcele, D., Lovett, M.C., and Norman, M.K. (2010). *How Learning Works: Seven Research-Based Principles for Smart Teaching.* Jossey-Bass.

[177] Bacon, D. R., & Stewart, K. A. (2006). How fast do students forget what they learn in consumer behavior? A longitudinal study. *Journal of Marketing Education,* 28(3), 181-192.

[178] Harboura K.E., Lauren L.E., Chris A.S.,& Lindsay E.H. (2015). A brief review of effective teaching practices that maximize student engagement, Preventing School Failure. *Alternative Education for Children and Youth,59*(1), 5–13.

[179] Nayir, F. (2017). The relationship between student movitivation and class engagement levels. *Eurasian Journal of Educational Research, 71,* 59–78.

[180] Vedder-Weiss, D., & Fortus, D. (2018). Teachers' mastery goals: Using a self-report survey to studty the relation between teaching practices and students' motivation for science learning. *Research in Science Education,* 48, 181–206.

[181] Kulik, J.A., Kulik, C.C., Bangert-Drowns, R.L. (1990). Is there better evidence on mastery learning? A response to Slavin. *Review of Educational Research, 60*(2), 303–307.

[182] Williams, T. (2017). Study: Nearly half of millennials get an 'F' in critical thinking. Goodcall. https://www.goodcall.com/news/critical-thinking-011043

[183] Williams, T. (2017). Study: Nearly half of millennials get an 'F' in critical thinking. Goodcall. https://www.goodcall.com/news/critical-thinking-011043

[184] Resnick, L. B. (2001). Making America Smarter: The real goal of school reform. In Costa, A.L. (Ed.), *Developing Minds: A Resource Book for Teaching Thinking,* 3–6. Association for Supervision and Curriculum Development.

[185] Schulz, H. & FitzPatrick, B. (2016). Teachers' understandings of critical and higher order thinking and what this means for their teaching and assessments. *Alberta Journal of Educational Research, 62*(1), 61–86.

[186] Nicholas, M.C., & Raider-Roth, M. (2016). A hopeful pedagogy to critical thinking. *International Journal for the Scholarship of Teaching and Learning, 10*(2), 1–10.

[187] Abrami, P.C. et al. (2008). Instructional interventions affecting critical thinking skills and sicpositions: A stage 1 meta-analysis. *Review of Educational Research, 78*(4), 1102–1134.

[188] Struyven, K., Doch, F., & Janssens, S. (2005). Students' perceptions about evaluation and assessment in higher education: A review. *Assessment & Evaluation in Higher Education, 30*(4), 325–341.

[189] Nicholas, M.C., & Raider-Roth, M. (2016). A hopeful pedagogy to critical thinking. *International Journal for the Scholarship of Teaching and Learning, 10*(2), 1–10.

[190] Nieto, A. M., & Saiz, C. (2008). Evaluation of Halpern's "structural component" for improving critical thinking. *The Spanish Journal of Psychology, 11*(1), 266–274.

[191] Halonen, J. S., Bosack, T., Clay, S., & McCarthy, M. (2003). A rubric for learning, teaching, and assessing scientific inquiry in psychol- ogy. *Teaching of Psychology, 30,* 196–208.

[192] McLean, C. P., & Miller, N. A. (2010). Changes in critical thinking skills following a course on science and pseudoscience: A quasi- experimental study. *Teaching of Psychology, 37,* 85–90.

[193] Abrami, P.C. et al. (2008). Instructional interventions affecting critical thinking skills and sicpositions: A stage 1 meta-analysis. *Review of Educational Research, 78*(4), 1102–1134.

[194] Liu, O. L., L. Frankel, and K. C. Roohr. (2014). Assessing Critical Thinking in Higher Edu- cation: Current State and Directions for Next-generation Assessment. *ETS Research Report* Series, i–23.

[195] Stellmack, M. A., Konheim-Kalkstein, Y. L., Manor, J. E., Massey, A. R., & Schmitz, J. A. (2009). An assessment of reliability and valid- ity of a rubric for grading APA-style introductions. *Teaching of Psychology, 36,* 102–107.

[196] Downing, K., Kwong, T., Chan, S., Lam, T, & Downing, W. (2009). Problem-based learning and the development of metacognition. *Higher Education, 57,* 609–621.

[197] Kuhn, D. (2000). Metacognitive development. *Current Direction in Psychological Science, 9*(5), 178–181.

[198] Renkl, A. & Atkinson, R.K.. (2003). Structuring the transition from example study to problem solving in cognitive skill acquisition: A cognitive load perspective. *Educational Psychologist, 38*(1), 15–22.

[199] Kahneman, D. (2011). *Thinking Fast and Slow.* Farrar, Straus and Giroux.

[200] Hartley, J., & Chesworth, K. (2010). Qualitative and quantitative methods in research on essay writing: no one way. *Journal of Further and Higher Education, 24*(1), 15–24.

[201] Hartley, J., & Chesworth, K. (2010). Qualitative and quantitative methods in research on essay writing: no one way. *Journal of Further and Higher Education, 24*(1), 15–24.

202   Evans, C. (2013). Making sense of assessment feedback in higher education. *Review of Educational Research, 83*(1), 70–120.

203   Boud, D., & Falchikov, N. (Eds.) (2007). Rethinking assessment in higher education. Routledge/Taylor Francis.

204   Orrel, J. (2006). Feedback on learning achievement: rhetoric and reality. *Teaching in Higher Education, 11,* 441–456.

205   West, J., & Turner, W. (2015). Enhancing the assessment experience: Improving student perceptions, engagement and understanding using online video feedback. *Innovations in Education and Teaching International, 53*(4), 400–410.

206   Marin, L.M., & Halpern, D.F. (2001). Pedagogy for developing critical thinking in adolescents: Explicit instruction produces greatest gains. *Thinking Skills and Creativity, 6*(1), 1–13.

207   Zakaria, F. (2016). *In Defense of a Liberal Education.* W. W. Norton. 74.

208   National Commission on Writing. (2003, April). *The neglected "r": The need for a writing revolution.* New York: The College Board.

209   Trimbur, J. (1994). Taking the social turn: Teaching writing post-process. *College Composition and Communication, 45*(1), 108–118.

210   Bazerman, C., & Tinberg, H. (2015). Writing is an expression of embodied cognition. In Adler-Kasser, L. & Wardle, E. (Eds.), *Naming what we know: Threshold concepts of writing studies* (pp. 74–75). Logan, UT: Utah State University Press.

211   Langer, S.K. (1979). *Philosophy in a New Key.* Harvard University Press.

212   Gillespie, A., Graham, S., Kiuhara, S., and Hebert, M. (2014). High school teachers use of writing to support students' learning: a national survey. *Reading and Writing, 27,* 1043–1072.

213   Townsend, M., Thompson, J.D.M., Anderman, L.H., & Wilton, K.M. (1993). Effects of introductions and conclusions in assessment of student essays. *Journal of Educational Psychology, 85*(4), 670–678.

CPSIA information can be obtained
at www.ICGtesting.com
Printed in the USA
BVHW030309100121
597335BV00002B/13